YOU
ONLY GET
MARRIED
FOR THE FIRST TIME ONCE

JUDY MARKEY

Takes On Natural Childbirth · Car Pools · Curfews · Saturday Nights · and All the Other Stuff That Threatens Your Already Shaky Sanity

NEW YORK · LONDON · TORONTO · SYDNEY · AUCKLAND

YOU

ONLY GET

MARRIED

FOR THE FIRST TIME ONCE

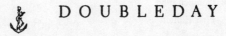 DOUBLEDAY

Published by Doubleday,
a division of Bantam Doubleday Dell
Publishing Group, Inc., 666 Fifth Avenue,
New York, New York 10103

Doubleday and the portrayal of an anchor with a dolphin
are trademarks of Doubleday, a division of Bantam
Doubleday Dell Publishing Group, Inc.

Library of Congress Cataloging-in-Publication Data

Markey, Judy.
    You only get married for the first time once : takes
on natural childbirth, nuclear families, car pools, curfews, miniskirts, Saturday nights, and all the other
stuff that threatens your already shaky sanity / Judy
Markey.—1st. ed.
        p. cm.
    1. Marriage—United States—Humor. 2. Parent-
hood—United States—Humor. 3. Family—United
States—Humor. 4. Sex—Humor.
I. Title.
HQ734.M344 1988
306.8'0207—dc19   88-9586
                                            CIP

BOOK DESIGN BY JULIE DUQUET

ISBN 0-385-24739-7

Printed in the United States of America
October 1988
First Edition
BG

For Erin and Adam—who have absolutely
no business growing up and learning to
drive and talk back and then leaving to go
off to college

ACKNOWLEDGMENTS

The hardest part about an acknowledgments page is trying to keep it from sounding like an Oscar speech. But I truly have bunches of people to thank. Not only the ones who believed from the beginning, like Mom, Carroll Stoner, and Mary Frances Veeck, but the ones who really made a difference these past few years, like Bob Page and Leslie Lewis and Dennie Allen and Bob Collins and Todd Musburger.

And then there are the folks who regularly loan me their lives to put on paper, like Chris and Jack Paschen, Alan and Janice Henry, Kathy O'Malley, Suzy Kellet, and the best brother in the world, Jim Lindheim.

And here comes the extra-special-thanks category— to Jean Naggar, Theresa Cavanaugh, and Loretta Barrett, the folks who really nurtured and birthed this book.

And last of all, my forever gratitude and love to the ones who put up with a less-than-wonderful me on a daily basis, Miss Erin, Mr. Adam, and—of course— Thomas.

TABLE OF CONTENTS

MAKING SURE THE KIDDIES HAVE ENOUGH MATERIAL FOR THEIR SHRINKS

BOOGYING WITH THE DAILY INSANITIES

GIRL NOTES

HOLIDAY BLISSES, MISSES, AND GET-ME-OUTTA-THIS-ES

NO, THERE AIN'T NO CURE FOR THE SUMMERTIME BLUES

MIXING IT UP WITH THE SEE-LEBS

YOU

ONLY GET

MARRIED

FOR THE FIRST TIME ONCE

INTRODUCTION

I'm just like you—slogging through the nutsiness out there and trying to stay afloat. Trying to pretend it's perfectly okay to live in a world where folks think a really swell gift idea is a bar of soap in the shape of a bagel. I mean we're all in this insanity together.

So I write for *us*. And I like being a writer. It's hard, but hey! so is being a mother. And columns almost never throw up, or make you buy them gerbils, or ask to have violin lessons. They just sit there. And they either work or they don't work.

I think the ones in this book really work. They were written over three years' time—years in which all sorts of bizarro things assaulted our former standards of normalcy—beepers, and pregnant dolls, and car phones, and hair mousse—but the reasons these columns hold up is most of them deal with the chronic issues that plague us.

Three times a week I grind out a column in which I try and make some sense of these issues. Not global issues. But everyday issues. Things like whatever happened to hickeys, and will sending a condolence letter ever get easier, and why does the average American child expect to be paid five bucks a week for doing no more than waking up and continuing to breathe, and how does this man expect me to be sexy when all he gives me for Christmas is an electric garage-door opener? The things that make us all froth at the mouth.

I write about those things—things that make us race to the

phone to call our best friend and begin to whine in a highly unattractive fashion. Only I try to get past the whining (gratifying though whining may be) and actually get some perspective on the deal. I figure that a columnist's job is clarification.

Clarification *and* consolation. Because it definitely helps a lot to know you aren't the only one in the world who bleeds when your seventh grader suddenly gets no phone calls for six months. And that you're not the only one in the world who gets completely grossed out when your husband uses your toothbrush—in spite of the fact that you have been doing far more disgusting things with this man for years.

Like I said, we're all in this together. Which is why my favorite letter to get is when someone says, "You write what I think." It's fun to hook into other people's heartbeats. To commiserate, to provoke, to get the laugh gland going.

And that's what this book is all about.

WHOSE BRIGHT IDEA WAS MARRIAGE, ANYWAY?

Advise and Dissent

There isn't a woman in the world whose marriage can survive more than one tennis lesson. Given by her husband.

This has nothing to do with tennis per se. Or even the woman and her husband per se. What it has to do with is the institution of marriage and what it does to the ability of one person to take directives from the other.

Somehow, once you are finally married to the person whose every breath once sent shivers up your spine, and whose every word once seemed oracular, some subtle, but significant, changes occur. These changes mark the beginning of the ancient and as yet unremedied phenomenon we refer to as the Spousal Credibility Plummet. Once this occurs, it becomes impossible to listen to any suggestions or receive any advice objectively from one's spouse.

You know it has set in when you begin to find it neither amusing, enlightening, nor endearing that your spouse has just said you're wearing your weights all wrong for your aerobics workout and he'd be happy to *show you how* to do it right.

There is a point in a relationship where the concept of *show you how* becomes an instantaneous invite to disaster. As in the above-mentioned *show you how* to play tennis. Or *show you how* to drive a stick shift. Or the ever-popular killer invite—*show you how* to play bridge. The wise woman knows: when you want someone to *show you how*, hire them, don't marry them. If God had not wanted us to learn skiing from ski instructors, he wouldn't have invented affairs.

Even more impossible than teaching skills to one's spouse is the attempt to offer advice. An idea posed by one's husband or wife has absolutely no clout. This has nothing to do with respect. You respect your spouse. But it's hard to give credence to a suggestion made by a person who you have, from time to time, seen ensconced on the commode. It always seems like an infinitely better idea if someone else—anyone else—but your lifesmate suggests it.

In our house we get around this by what we refer to as the Michael Duhl Maneuver. Michael Duhl is married to one of my friends. He is very smart. But no smarter than the man I personally selected as my forever companion down the rocky road of life. The point is, however, Michael Duhl is *not* my forever companion. This gives him a credibility quotient significantly higher than anyone to whom I might be matrimonially related.

Thus, when my lifesmate wants to offer me counsel, he employs the Michael Duhl Maneuver. Say, for instance, he wants to propose what he considers to be a sterling suggestion. He knows full well that as soon as he puts forth this idea I would first bristle, then say, "Are you kidding?" and then snort with great hauteur. I am especially great at the snorting part.

So instead he calls Michael Duhl and tells him the idea. Michael in turn calls me, and I in turn tell him it's absolutely brilliant. The system is foolproof. And as a public service I offer it up to you. The Michael Duhl Maneuver works for everyone.

Except, of course, Mrs. Michael Duhl.

So do spindle beds. Spindle beds went out years ago. There must have been a reason for this. One reason is that unless you are Wilt Chamberlain or the Jolly Green Giant, a spindle bed requires either a large leap or a small ladder for liftoff and entry. Another reason is the noise factor. Spindle beds have probably the most vehement, most rackety, most braying system of springs under them this side of the Clamorous Contraption Hall of Fame. We are talking major deafening groans every time you make a move. Even the most benign move, like turning from your stomach to your side, emits a ruckus so obstreperous and lusty that it would seem to be caused by nothing short of the most depraved carnal activities.

Which brings us to the ever-popular subject of carnal activities. There are two kinds in country inns with charme. Your carnal activities and the carnal activities of the folks in the room next door. The problem is it gets hard to tell them apart. Country inns with charme do not have noise-muffling rugs. They have bare floors. Country inns with charme do not have noise-muffling insulation. They have skinny—albeit original—nineteenth-century walls. Country inns with charme do not have privacy.

What this means is you just paid forty bucks for the privilege of having to mute all the sexy noises you could have muted for free at home. Of course at home you wouldn't have had the flipside privilege of bearing auditory witness to the decadence going on in the room next door. And there is plenty. Because they came there for the same reason you did. And it wasn't just to go antiquing. It is a very bizarre experience to be privy to the sexual soundtrack of two total strangers. There is nothing to do but wait it out, and try to keep the visuals you are imagining somewhere in the realm of softcore rather than hardcore. After all, you're going to have to face these anonymous voluptuaries at breakfast the next morning.

That, of course, is the pièce de résistance part of country inns with charme. You get to go down for coffee and wonder which one of the three other couples there (who all look like central casting versions of librarians and Santa Clauses) were the ones moaning "Oh please, please, don't stop" but a few short hours before. The whole experience is very taxing.

Which is why at 8:05 the next morning your check directly

Ye Olde Charme

The whole point was to have a romantic weekend in the country. You wanted a respite from the contemporary din, an atmospheric retreat. So after major research you come up with Just The Place. It was a nineteenth-century inn, on a pond, in the woods—one of those joints drenched in charm. Only at this sort of joint they spell charm like this: charme. The extra e should have been the tipoff.

Because what happens when you head for the joints that graft on the extra e is you pay dearly for the e and all the other olde world adorabilities. And the room they showed you to was reeking with olde world adorability. First of all, it was one of four rooms on the top floor of a coach house. Look darling!—dormer windows! How cozy.

What you didn't know from cozy. Second of all, it was on the top floor with three other bedrooms and . . . two other baths. Get it? Four bedrooms, two baths? You get to share. For forty bucks a night you get the privilege of being confronted by the toothpaste droppings and sink hairs of total strangers. Not to mention being within earshot of all their scatalogical efforts. Unfortunately, when people try to underscore the point of basic human equality by saying even the queen of England goes to the bathroom, you are not among those who find this a particularly reassuring image. You prefer to think of royalty fully clothed and in a more dignified stance. You prefer to think of strangers in the same fashion. Shared bathrooms tend to make that impossible.

the more they do that, the stronger their feelings of love and closeness.

For instance, the study says that nicknames like "Caveman" and "Piglet" can heighten a couple's feelings of intimacy. And it even said that using coy little euphemisms like "Puppies" and "Bibbles" for body parts actually strengthens romantic bonds.

Oh swell.

And just my luck I read this truly barf-ola scientific info just before my twentieth anniversary. An anniversary my husband and I had somehow managed to reach in spite of never nuzzling each other in a movie theater or whispering sweet nothings to each other while attending dinner parties for eight.

Of course, true to form, we were celebrating this occasion under less than candlelight conditions, anyway, considering that on our actual anniversary we were escorted into the last available room of an upstate New York inn—a room that had two single beds.

Twenty years before, the two of us would have wedged ourselves into one of them. But what's the point of being married twenty years if you can't opt for a decent night's sleep?

I took the bed by the door and Caveman and his bibbles took the bed by the window.

Sweet Nothings

There's only one thing worse than going out with another couple that fights in front of you. And that's going out with another couple that foreplays in front of you.

You know the kind of folks I mean. They are the ones who—no matter where they are and who they're with—are fiercely determined to win the Hottest Couple of the Evening Award. They are the ones who can't reach for peanuts without stopping to touch each other's hands, who can't finish a sentence without looking meaningfully into each other's eyes. They are the ones who take courses *together*.

You hate these couples. And you always exit from an evening with them thinking three things: 1) They obviously need to do this in order to make you feel you have a substandard marriage. 2) What if you *do* have a substandard marriage? 3) They probably do, too. They probably shut down their whole hormonal hype machine as soon as they get home. You just know she pulls on a flannel nightgown and acquires a severe headache and he is in fact relieved about both. You just know it.

So here's the bad news. Thought Number 3 ain't true, because I just read a study saying that these couples, couples that pillow talk in public, actually go home and pillow talk in private. This study said if you are out with a couple that calls each other sexy nicknames, that whispers little innuendo-y things to each other at a party, that talks to each other in some sort of conjugal code, that out of the country inn with charme and check right into the local Sheraton. When it comes to a great romantic weekend, you'll take avocado shag carpeting, a hard queen-size bed, and your very own wrapped, sanitized toilet any day.

Dee-Vorce: A Macro View

Granted I fall somewhere between John Kenneth Galbraith and Gracie Allen in my overall grasp of economics. But I see terrifying economic times approaching. Here's why . . .

Divorces are declining. For twenty years they had been on the increase and then, starting a few years ago, people began sticking out their marriages. This may be swell for the American family, but it could be the death knell for the American economy.

No one has probably ever had the nerve to say this yet, but divorce is one of the mainstays of the American economy. And I'm not talking lawyers. I'm not talking shrinks. I'm talking fundamental GNP.

There is hardly a major industry in America that doesn't do a whole lot better when a marriage falls asunder. Let's start with Detroit. According to recent statistics, the average American household has 1.5 cars. Thus as long as Mom and Dad are still doing the Mister and Misses bit, most of us get by on less than two motor vehicles. After all, Mom and Dad are both headed to the same pizza joint on Saturday night. But once Mom and Dad split up, depending on who got the station wagon, somebody is in the market for a car. Dee-troit loves dee-vorce.

So does Hollywood. Everyone knows a dad doesn't know how to talk to his kid. When he's married, it doesn't matter. Mom is there to do the communicating. But once a dad starts being in charge of a whole kid for a whole weekend, what else is he going to do but take the kid to the movies? Otherwise he might have to relate to him. Not to mention, now that a divorced mom and her husband aren't fighting in front of the entire bridge club, what's she going to do on yet another dateless Saturday night but rent a movie? The film industry is absolutely dependent on divorce.

So is the diet industry. A recent Weight Watchers survey revealed that the average woman respondent put on twenty-three pounds during thirteen years of marriage and the average man put on eighteen pounds in the same amount of time. Marriage is very fattening. However, when you're married, you can live with fat. Most of those men said their interest in sex was undiminished by their wives' weight gain. However, when you're divorced, the larded look is not a major attribute on the old attractiveness charts. Where would the $5-billion weight-loss industry be if marriages didn't break up?

Then there's the airline industry. I have a friend who used to put her kid on Capitol Air's sub-cheapo flight out to L.A. once a month to see Daddy. The plane was crammed with other little broken-home kidlets heading west for their weekend with their noncustodial parent. For years Capitol did a booming business in shuttling these junior jet-setters between Mom and Dad. So what happens? 1984 was the first year divorce rates plummeted. And only a few short months later, Capitol was out of business.

Therefore, fellow citizens, I urge you to take action now. Your country's economic future is at stake. Staying married is tantamount to sabotage. Think twice before deciding not to get divorced.

And let us all remember the words of that great patriot Mickey Rooney: "I regret that I have but eight marriages to give for my country."

On Buttons and Betrayals

Buttons are bad for relationships. Not the kind of buttons that come with buttonholes, but the kind that go on commonly found technological items.

For instance, the buttons on your resident VCR. Recently I asked the man I personally selected to be my lifesmate to do me a favor. It was not a large favor. It was not a difficult favor. It was not a time-consuming favor. All I asked the man was to set the button on the VCR to tape one evening's episode of a twelve-hour miniseries I'd become embroiled in. Any dork with a 92 IQ could have done it. I, of course, did not marry a dork. He, of course, forgot.

Calm was not how I felt about this. I felt that when a person has invested eight entire hours of her life in a miniseries, for her beloved to deprive her of the pivotal ninth and tenth hours is tantamount to saying, "Ha ha, you have just blown eight entire hours—the equivalent of a full day's work—for nothing, you big sucker." You cannot jump back into a miniseries at the eleventh hour. You can, however, give serious consideration to divorce.

The second set of buttons that was recently used against me was on my car radio. Let me start this by saying there is not much in a woman's life that is sacrosanct. Especially if that woman lives in a house with a teenaged womanette who feels she is perfectly entitled to "borrow" that woman's only unrusted razor, and "lend" that woman's Eagles tapes to her little womanette friends. What are moms for, if not to be pillaged?

Thus you will frequently find the mom of a womanette retreating to her car for solace, this being the only place in which she can be pretty sure that everything will remain just as she left it. Such as the steering wheel being in the same place on the steering column and all. Moms find this reassuring. What is not reassuring is that one day their local department of motor vehicles actually deems it legal for the womanette to drive the mom's personal car on the highways and byways of America. What is even less reassuring is the lightning speed with which a womanette commits the ultimate unspeakable act: The kid resets the mom's radio buttons.

It is the final defilement. A woman can take almost anything except five rhythm 'n' puke, counterculture radio stations. A woman gets into her car expecting to have pushbutton access to the news. She gets into her car expecting to have pushbutton access to Lionel Richie. She gets into her car expecting to have pushbutton access to National Public Radio. A woman should not be expected to give any of that up. But of course she has to. The womanette is a new driver. And she absolutely needs the coolest possible music on during every given moment of vehicle driving.

One knows enough not to argue. One knows enough not to try and placate the womanette with a mere two buttons. One knows if one does that, instead of watching the road, the womanette will be watching the dial trying to hunt up the rest of her music. Thus, in order to keep the kid in a breathing format, the woman gives up her last five radio buttons.

Of course they're never really her last. She's a woman. She's a wife. She's a mom. It's always possible to find a few more buttons of hers to push.

Uh, This Is My . . .

The problem is getting worse. According to a recent Census Bureau report, the number of unmarried couples living together IN SIN has more than tripled since 1970. The problem is not the IN SIN part—the problem still is how does one refer to the person who he or she happens to live with, happens to sleep with, happens to fight with, but just hasn't happened to marry?

This is not a new dilemma. But it seems to be the Ultimately Unresolvable Social Quandry of the Late Twentieth Century. Etiquette experts from Miss Post to Miss Manners have been grappling with it for well over a decade and as yet have not come up with anything even resembling a solution. Major semantics sweepstakes have been held in the hopes that some creative wizard would come up with the *mot juste* to describe a couple of liaison-ees, but all their efforts are either arid ("householdmate"), cumbersome ("significant cohabitant"), or saccharine beyond belief ("the woman I love and live with").

The problem is not that there is a paucity of descriptives in our national vocabulary, it's that there is an absurd insistence that we explain ourselves, our living arrangements, our long- and our short-term goals, and our three favorite positions to almost everybody. In days of yore, there used to be an operative concept called "discretion." When discretion was in vogue, people were fooling around about as much as they do today, but they felt considerably less compelled to cram that fact into an introduction. Now we've gone and complicated our private sex life with public apartment leases and that, combined with our compulsion for candor, is what got us into this ridiculous verbal impasse.

So we are left with three options. The first is an array of dopey descriptives that should be banished from the vocabulary of anyone over 15.7 years old. But there we are saying, "This is my old lady" (which makes us sound like we haven't left Berkeley or gotten out of our Kris Kristofferson phase); "This is my girlfriend" (which is even worse because we sound like we're triple dating with Wally and the Beaver); or "This is my roomie" (which sounds like any one of ten sitcoms featuring oddly mixed, but healthy, heterosexual groupings).

Option number two is the mix-and-match couplings of words like "significant," "meaningful," "other," "consequential," "one," "partner," and "relationship." Occasionally we even make the heinous error of also trying to weave a "committed" in there, although surveys bear out that the inclusion of this word by the introducer is never anything less than real nauseating to both the introduced and the introduce-ee.

And then there's option number three. It's a last resort but it does solve the problem. Since we apparently can't find the *prose* solution, we may have to consider going with the *prosaic* solution— just shut up and marry him or her. It won't make your life much more complicated than it already is, and it will be a whole lot simpler when it comes to introductions.

"This is my *wife.*" You might even get to like the sound of it.

Rent-a-Hubby

How's this for a great little business concept . . . Rent-a-Husband?

Okay, I admit I got the idea from a New Jersey lady who invented an actual business called Rent-a-Wife, a business that has really taken off. And what's particularly interesting about it is that 75 percent of her clients are women. So I figure, if there are folks willing to pay $10 to $15 per hour to rent themselves a wife, surely there must be a market just as willing to plunk down $15 per hour in order to rent a husband.

Just think of all the incredibly valuable things husbands are good for . . .

Now wait a minute. That's not funny. Of course there are bunches of things husbands are good for. It just takes a minute to sit down and gather our thoughts for this.

Okay. Maybe it'll be easier if we eliminate some things. You know, the things husbands are *not* good for, even though they think they are. Like fixing things. Men seem to operate under the illusion that they are innately gifted in dealing with all things electronic, mechanical, and otherwise. So they all have big red toolboxes downstairs in the basement attesting to their readiness to tackle any technological emergency that may surface. Next to those big red boxes are the innards of trillions of defunct toaster ovens, clock radios, and portable tape recorders. Next to those are instructions in various foreign languages that have been crumpled during fits of pique, into balls of many sizes. And next to those is a large box of tissues. They use them to wipe away the tears.

Another thing husbands are not too swell at is mastering the digital intricacies of a VCR. Of course, in all fairness, wives aren't too swell at this, either. If you need help with a VCR, it's probably best to call Rent-a-Kid.

But let's return to the Rent-a-Husband concept and our list of all the services a husband provides.

Things like spider-killing. I think it has to be acknowledged that men are significantly less likely to panic when it comes to disposing of God's little many-legged critters.

Husbands are also quite good with garbage. And apparently they put great value on their garbage-hauling services. Otherwise, why would they feel that 4.2 minutes of garbage hauling entitles them to breakfast, dinner, and clean laundry services for an entire week?

And you have to admit it's pretty important to have one of them around when you want to instigate The Silent Treatment.

Another thing I have always found particularly valuable in husbands is their ability to explain the meaning of "arbitrage."

They also have great razors.

So you figure it out. Considering the frequency with which we tend to annihilate a spider, shave our legs, and inquire about arbitrage, well, you can just imagine the kind of need there would be out there for Rent-a-Husband.

At fifteen bucks an hour, you could be rich by 2988.

Love and the Loo

In a world obsessed by trivia, it is hardly surprising that a recent survey has just brought us the following vital facts and figures: 40 percent of the American male population reads while on the toilet; 20 percent smokes while similarly situated; 14 percent listens to the radio; and—get this—8 percent talks on the phone. (Somehow, we have been spared being made privy—no pun intended—to the same set of statistics for American women.)

Actually, this survey, which seems both superfluous and shocking at the same time, is somewhat thought-provoking because bathroom attitudes and activities are very revealing of the psychological workings of a person. There are those who swear the key to our quirks is environment; there are those who swear the key to our quirks is heredity; but there are some who realize that it's comportment in the WC that most reflects an individual's needs and neuroses.

Basically, there are two kinds of people. Those who absolutely savor their time in there and those who deal with it briskly. It is hard for those in the latter category to comprehend the relish with which some members of the populace regard those moments in their porcelain paradise. But there are actually people who meticulously select their magazine for reading, methodically sharpen their pencils for the crossword, and precisely line up the right FM station for listening before any attention can be paid to Mother Nature. Then they just settle in for a great time.

Of course the major attraction of the latrine is that it's the only spot in the house offering even a modicum of seclusion. This isn't only true for mothers whose children never leave them alone, but this is also true for children whose mothers never leave them alone. Think about it. More than any other room in the house, it was in the white-tiled privacy of the bathroom that some of our very major rites of passage took place—it is where we smoked our first cigarette, unraveled the mysteries of tampons, and applied our first globs of Clearasil. For most of us, bathrooms are rife with memorable emotional epiphanies.

But more importantly, a bathroom is where we have the luxury of being our least refined self. Which is why so many people have such a tough time letting someone they love see them in such an uncouth state. There are people who have been married for decades, who have probably performed all sorts of less than aesthetic acts with each other, and yet they have never permitted their spouse to enter, and would never consider walking in on their significant other, when the bathroom door is closed. There's intimacy . . . and there's intimacy. Some think it's impolite; some think it's immoral; and some think it's nothing short of immensely obscene. I have a friend who takes the sanctity of bathroom solitude so seriously that she actually closes the john door even when she's home alone. And the thing is, she is not a starched, buttoned-up type. She has gone topless at a Club Med, she has seen three of Marilyn Chambers finer X-rated films, and she does not go all blushy if the jokes get a bit gamey. But she has never let her husband of eighteen years into the locked confines of the lavatory when it happens to be her turn. She is absolutely adamant that communal commode-ing is death to a relationship.

I don't agree. Seems to me that the ultimate cement of a relationship is still being crazy about the person after they've gone and burped (or worse) in your presence. It isn't a question of flaunting our gastrointestinal goings-on, but life has enough pretension and camouflage without having to carry it over into the domain of basic biological functions. Who are we kidding if we close the door? Indignities are an inherent part of life.

I know this goes counter to the moon/spoon/June school of romantic ecstasy, but the truth is that you know he *really* loves you, not when he hands you the ring, but when he hands you the roll of Charmin.

Risky Conversational
Business

A new study tells us that married couples talk to each other approximately thirty minutes a week. This includes the parts where you say "Pass the salt" and "Where's the sports section?" Thirty minutes. Everybody seems real shocked over this.

Not me. I'm just shocked—and mighty concerned—that married couples spend even that long communicating. Because even though all the shrinks tell us to communicate, anyone who has ever been married knows that talking is real risky. Too much conversation can be very hazardous to a relationship.

Let me explain why. In the beginning of a relationship there is lots to find out about the other person. How he feels about Hunan versus Szechuan, for instance. Whether or not he thinks a dictionary is fair to use when doing a crossword puzzle. Sorting these things out takes a lot of discourse. And provides many wonderful hours of interpersonal discoveries.

However, there are just so many interpersonal discoveries that can be made between two people before you start running out of material. What I mean by that is unless you are a particulary deep person, most of us have, say, X number of impassioned, witty, or insightful observations to impart. I'm not saying here that you are shallow. Well, yes I am, but then no more shallow than the rest of us. And I am saying that after a certain number of years with another person, you pretty much know how he feels about the job, or about life after death, or about compulsory seat-belt laws.

Which means that in order to have something resembling an actual conversation, you start talking about things you have no business talking about. Such as money. Or how to discipline the kids. Two topics guaranteed to land the average American couple in the divorce court of their choice.

So, in order to avoid that, you find yourself scrounging around for topics that transcend the mundane aspects of money and/or kids. Therefore, in an effort to come up with a meaningful conversation, one of you might say . . .

• "Now answer me honestly. I promise not to get mad. Have you found our relationship to be really fulfilling?"

• "I'm not saying I'd accept or anything, but if the boss asked me to run the office in Toadsuck, Arkansas, how would you feel about picking up stakes?"

• "Can I ask you something? If my old boyfriend/girlfriend called me for lunch, would you be jealous?"

Well you can just imagine what hits the fan when one of those discussions gets under way. Old grievances are aired, new ones are created, blame is assigned, invectives are hurled, and everyone leaves the battlefield bleeding and wounded.

Therefore, if you want to keep your marriage intact, I'd suggest cutting back on those thirty minutes of conversation a week. I'd suggest fifteen minutes. Tops. My theory is, if you love 'em, don't talk to 'em. Because if you don't talk, you don't fight. And if you don't fight, you don't have to apologize. And as we all know . . . loving someone is never having to say you're you-know-what.

The Forty-Eight-Hour Sulk

"**S**o how's Marlene?" I inquired of Mr. Marlene.

"How should I know?" he replied, brimming with exasperation. "She's not talking to me. She's in the twenty-seventh hour of a Forty-Eight-Hour Sulk."

God, what great news. A woman who has the nerve to sulk again. Sulking has gone out of favor during this past decade as a viable tactic in your basic marital dispute. That's because it became so terribly chic to *vent*. And suppressed anger (absolutely vital to fuel a quality Forty-Eight-Hour Sulk) was no longer permissible. The whole theory was to let the rancor flow. Books entitled *It's Fun to Be Furious*, *The Happy Hollerer*, *The Anger Principle*, and *The One-Minute Rage* glutted our shelves and tried to convince us that purging was a more constructive approach than pouting.

Well, were they wrong. The Forty-Eight-Hour Sulk is back. And for a very good reason. It is ultimately one of the most gratifying options available in the marital-altercation arsenal. Thus, for those of you married in the last decade who, as victims of the venting philosophy, have never experienced the exquisite pleasures of long-term pouting, we would like to outline the myriad advantages of the Forty-Eight-Hour Sulk.

First of all, venting anger doesn't begin to give that sweet sense of self-righteousness that even a modestly talented sulker can work himself or herself up to. (Please note: Contrary to popular opinion, The Great Sulk is not the exclusive domain of the female of the species. History has shown some sensational sulking—(i.e., freezing out of others, sanctimonious airs—can be achieved equally well by those of the male persuasion—Richard Nixon comes immediately to mind.)

But I digress. Once you've spewed your wrath, it can be pretty embarrassing. But if you quietly continue to nuture your rage, dignity, nay, piety, is yours. Consider the proverbial hairs-on-the-bathroom-sink issue. Scream at someone about how furious it makes you that he never wipes off the sink, and you sound like a shrew. If you calmly confront him in your most therapy-ized demeanor and quietly announce that you'd like to *share* with him that those hairs make you *hostile*, you sound very petty. Even worse you sound like you come from California. But say nothing for two days and silently suffer the demeaning task of wiping his hair from the bathroom sink, and you have a major moral edge. It's one of the more delicious aspects of sulking.

Sulking also serves to extend the length of even the most modest altercation. Ten minutes after you've vented, what are you left with? Post-fight-'em blues. Quelle letdown. But a Forty-Eight-Hour Sulk is the perfect solution for dragging these things out to a satisfactory duration.

Additionally there's a certain elegance, a certain *je ne sais quoi* to the well-honed sulk. Venting encourages shabby behavior such as plate throwing and cutlery waving. And at its worst, venting forces you to undertake outrageous deeds simply for dramatic effect. Suddenly are you packing a suitcase as if you were Claudette Colbert throwing half her closet (hangers included) into a ready valise and William Wyler had written you a great exit line. Only he hasn't. And you feel like something of a toad with all your sweat suits stuffed into your duffel and with nowhere to go. No, the Forty-Eight-Hour Sulk is infinitely more dignified than that.

Of course the best thing about these sulks is that you just slip out of them at the forty-eighth hour. No apologies are necessary. You're simply ready to behave like a human being again. And you are perfectly willing to continue behaving that way—until the next time the jerk pisses you off.

Take One Forehead,
Affix Gold Star

If you've been married more than an hour and a half, it's pretty hard to resist reading an article entitled "Why Marriages Last." Because already you should be nervous. Or if not nervous, at least wondering.

In a recent issue of *Psychology Today* there is a "Why Marriages Last" article with a list of the top fifteen reasons three hundred long-lasting couples think their unions have endured. Most of the reasons are fairly predictable, and women and men seem to rank them in the same order. But about two thirds of the way down the list a really striking thing occurs . . .

Number ten on the men's list is "I am proud of my spouse's achievements." Women don't even say "I am proud of my spouse's achievements" until their very last reason.

What do you make of that? Well, your first reaction, if you haven't purged yourself of all that strident feminism from yesteryear, might be to bristle and think, Boy, does that ever reek of patronization. You know, look at little Mimsey; not only did she raise Junior and Tammy Ann, but isn't she cute with her little blazer and briefcase going off to her little part-time job every morning. Gol-ly, isn't that little gal something? But I hardly think that's what most men are saying here.

They're saying just what it sounds like they're saying. That they genuinely are pleased with whatever it is the women in their lives have set out to do. Contrary to popular opinion, there are a whole lot of men out there who, instead of being threatened by their wives' accomplishments, are truly respectful, delighted, and not a little dazzled.

I married one of those guys. And I know for sure that whether I decided to go for the cleanest house on the block or win a Pulitzer prize or break 100 in golf, he would have looked up at me about one Thursday night a month and said, "You know, I really am proud of what you've done." Because he does that a lot. And I smile, and say thank you, and feel lucky.

Only I don't say it back. And according to that survey, most other women don't either. Why don't we tell our husbands that we are proud of what they have done? I suppose it has to do with expectations. At some fundamental level, many of us still haven't really transcended the basic Neanderthal mentality which dictates that it's his fundamental responsibility to provide.

So regardless of the dollars on the paycheck, or the grief he may endure in the office, or the relentless pressure of knowing that the bulk of economic responsibility probably will always fall on him, for the most part we don't issue a whole lot of appreciation or accolades. We just figure that whatever he's accomplished, he's more or less supposed to accomplish, and we don't often stop to tell him how proud we are that he has actually accomplished it. Perhaps some of us feel that by telling him he's doing a great job, he might begin to think that he has the option not to do a great job. Or perhaps some of us are just being a little bit withholding.

In any case, I think it wouldn't kill us to lean over and tell the guy we're proud of him too . . . it being a nice little un-Father's Day gift and all.

Money: His, Hers, and What You Thought Was Ours

Ladies and gentlemen. Once again it is time to bring you a wonderful tale of turned tables. So sit back, relax, and enjoy The Irony Hour.

This week, The Irony Hour brings you a saga from the eternally dicey domain of intracouple finances. As anyone who is one half of a couple knows, there is almost no topic as likely to put you on the battlefield as money. Religion is too abstract, politics is too boring, and sex is too nonexistent to argue over. But money is a piece of cake. It triggers all sorts of slimy things—things like power, manipulation, and the ever-popular issue of control.

Money, of course, has always been wonderful fodder for marital discord. For instance, during those bygone days of yesteryear, when the guys put on their Daddy-hats and went out to bring home the bacon, the basic perception was that there was a provider and a providee. Thus, the arguments that tended to ensue usually focused on the providee spending a tad too much of what the provider brought home. Lucy and Ricky Ricardo ("Lucy! Whass thees bill for three pair of peenk shoos?") filled our TV screens with this stuff for years.

But with more and more couples becoming two-income couples, the stakes have grown higher and the complications thicker. Now the breakdown gets a bit nastier. Now there are two providers who—unless a monetary miracle has occurred—do not *ever* earn the same salary. This means that one is the richer (let that translate into smug, manipulative, and sanctimonious) and one is the poorer (let that translate into defensive and somewhat neurotic).

Because of this richer/poorer discrepancy many households operate with a convoluted system of economic distribution. This system generally goes under the heading of His Money, Her Money, and Our Money. This is very modern. And the illusion is that this system offers both fairness and freedom. Fairness because each partner puts into the pot according to his or her income, and freedom because he or she is then free to spend a day at Elizabeth Arden or drop $100 on new fishing tackle and not have to justify it to a soul. Especially the soul to whom he or she is married.

Which is all well and good until the U.S. Postal Service interferes. It seems in the modern marriage of Sally and Richard a notice from Richard's bank arrived the other day. The notice was an annual tally of Richard's His Money account. A notice never meant for little Sally's eyes. Especially since Richard had managed to stash $2,000 in there during the past three months.

Sally saw that $2,000 figure and went insane. She felt betrayed and enraged and convinced that the guy was a rotter because obviously he was earning more money than he owned up to. This is, of course, the ultimate betrayal in the modern marriage. Better she should have found pictures of him and a bimbo in a motel than that he was holding out on her. Richard explained that his stash was merely a fifth week's salary from the past two months plus some racetrack winnings. Sally was not assuaged.

Richard spent the weekend Xeroxing his check stubs and getting his records in order. Sally is demanding an audit.

Thus we have come full circle. Once the Lucys of the world had to defend spending their money to their husbands. Now the Richards have to defend saving their money to their wives.

Have we come a long way, baby, or what?

50-50 Does Not
Equal Make

I believe they call themselves . . . Egalitarian Couples. I've been reading "How We Became an Egalitarian Couple" articles for a few years in all the $1.95 magazines that tell you how to live your life better. Basically what they say is that it's possible to have an "equal-partner marriage." For those of us who have regularly rankled at the seeming inequities in our marriage partnership, this is of course a very intriguing concept.

Egalitarian Coupledom is based on the conviction that all tedious chores (from laundry folding to raking the leaves to buying the goat cheese to paying Ma Bell) are divisible along non-boy/non-girl lines, and can be distributed EQUALLY between two comradely adults who take their egalitarian status seriously. And make no mistake about it, these equal-partnership people take the fundamental 50-50 split of choredom very seriously. You ain't seen seriously until you hear the gravity with which the EC's tackle the whose-turn-is-it-to-go-to-the-cleaner question.

Here's how it works (as documented in the magazines—not in real life. I am convinced there could only be about 6.2 EC couples in real life). Charlotte gets home from the office at 6:06. Basil has been home all day. He is a writer so he works at home. Which in the old-fashioned working-wife situation would mean that even though she's been at the office all day, Charlotte gets to do the laundry, start the dinner, and fetch the cleaning. And which in the supposedly modern house-husband situation would mean that in addition to being a writer, Basil also would get to do the laundry, start the dinner, and fetch the cleaning. But he did none of the above. That's because this is an equal partnership and Basil did the laundry and started the dinner and fetched the cleaning all last week. This is Char's week. But . . . guess what Char has been doing on her lunch hour all week? Typing Basil's manuscript. Which has to be worth a fistful of trips to the cleaner, the way Char sees it. Not so to Basil. After all, didn't he spend two hours waiting in line this week so they could get good seats for the ballet *she* was *dying* to see. That's gotta be worth something, too. So what the EC couple does is sit down, discuss, evaluate, and negotiate the cleaner issue.

Because with EC couples *everything* is an issue. Here is a direct quote from one of the radiantly happy EC converts, in *Esquire* magazine last year: "Every aspect of daily life has to be worked out; nothing is left to habit, nothing is left undiscussed." Equal-partnership marriages have raised belaboring to an absolute art form. In the time they spend weighing, deliberating, and delegating, they could have run to the 7-Eleven twice and back. Instead what they do is take twenty minutes to figure out that it really wouldn't be fair if one went and the other got to stay home, so they both go to the store and waste another twenty minutes each. Which means a grand total of eighty human-minutes have been spent knocking off a twenty-minute task. Of course every now and then they throw caution to the wind and say, What the hell, honey, even though it's your turn to cook tonight, I'll make the gazpacho, and you can read me all the dirt from the *National Enquirer*. Now that's a chunk of magnaminity.

Which, of course, is one of eighty-seven drawbacks to the whole egalitarian concept. If everything is perceived in an I'll-scratch-yours-if-you'll-scratch-mine mindset, whither goes spontaneity and basic goodwill? If every time Harvey makes the bed, Mrs. Harvey knows it's gonna cost her something down the road, it sort of leeches generosity and giving-ness out of the marriage. Scoreboarding the dopey tasks of life is ultimately a demeaning and very exhausting endeavor.

No thanks. I'd rather continue in my nonegalitarian, unequal partnership marriage any day. I may be doing more than my share, but there's a wonderful advantage to that. At least that way I get to be a martyr.

Intracouple Impasse

Nobody's marriage or meaningful relationship has ever crumbled because the tube of toothpaste wasn't squeezed from the bottom. But that clichéd, mangled tube is the perfect example of a sociological phenomenon I have uncovered in my most recent unscientific survey—the Intracouple Impasse.

You will be relieved to note that the Intracouple Impasse is exactly what it sounds like. It is the one issue between two people on which no one is willing to budge. I'm not talking sweeping political/philosophical issues like abortion or nuclear armament. I'm talking puny, mundane, almost-beneath-your-dignity-to-even-acknowledge issues like ice trays and toilet-paper rolls.

Surely in the annals of Intracouple Impasses, none is more common than the great toilet-paper-roll standoff. It would appear that in a majority of American couples there is always one partner who is totally incapable of (1) noticing a roll is empty, (2) doing something about it. This lack of skill might be considered by some —especially the partner who is doing 100 percent of the toilet-paper-roll changing—as less an ineptitude than perhaps a clear case of passive/aggressive behavior. Whatever it is, no one has come up with an all-purpose solution to the toilet-paper trauma. One woman told me that fortunately she has three bathrooms in her home, so she just moves from one to the other. But ultimately, even she runs out of bathrooms and is indeed forced to change rolls.

However, when this happens, she retaliates in kind. For some reason her husband, who is totally indifferent to his supply of Charmin, is absolutely fastidious about his supply of butter. He apparently insists on cutting it from just one end of the stick. Thus, every time this woman has finished changing three rolls of toilet paper, she goes to the butter dish and gouges out a nice chunk from the wrong end. This makes her feel much better.

Next consider the shirt-button standoff. Daniel has three shirts that are perfectly good. Except they each need a button. They have needed these buttons for seven years. In the last seven years Daniel and Karen have moved from Boston to Philadelphia to Chicago. Each time they move Daniel solemnly folds, packs up, ships, and unpacks these three unwearable shirts. Karen refuses to sew on the buttons. Daniel refuses to learn how to sew on the buttons. He says that's not the point. He says that then the shirts lose their value to both of them. For Karen those buttonless shirts mean she is sticking by her principles. And for Daniel those buttonless shirts mean he is entitled to feel a bit shortchanged, a bit self-righteous. Something like this is really quite rare—both partners refuse to budge, and yet both feel better. Surely this is the I.I.I.—the Ideal Intracouple Impasse.

My favorite I.I., however, came from a couple in Cleveland. The full Cleveland treatment in I.I.s is really quite impressive. It's the old soap in the shower I.I. Even if he is down to the last three slivers of ossified soap, Carol's husband absolutely refuses to open a new bar and bring it into the shower. Therefore Carol always opens it. But it gets her real ticked off. So after she dries off, she takes the new bar with her and hides it.

Cleanliness is *not* always next to Godliness.

Tipping the
Conjugal Scale

The deal you made was "in sickness and in health, for richer for poorer, for better for worse." Nowhere did it say for "fatter or thinner." And yet in thirteen years of marriage, the average woman gains twenty-three pounds and the average man gains eighteen. Marriage can really ruin a fiancée's figure.

If husband and wife pork up at about the same rate, as in those Weight Watchers survey figures above, the situation would be simple: The couple could either continue to wallow around in their expanded corporal confines, or they could decide to diet and whittle away their expanded corporal confines. BUT . . . if one decides to diet and the other continues to wallow—or if one doesn't need to diet while the other continues to wallow, then you have a serious problem. Real serious.

Barry and Suzanne are at the marriage counselor. For the past year she has been driving the man crazy because he won't/can't/hasn't shed the twenty pounds he's put on during their fifteen-year marriage. His belly has become their major battlefield.

Barry knows his belly is there, but with the right tailoring and the right jacket it's barely noticeable. Barry just sees himself as "a big guy." Men do that. An article in the current issue of the *Journal of Abnormal Psychology* reports both men and women distort their body images, but *most women distort their body images negatively,* seeing themselves in worse shape than they are, and *most men distort their perceptions positively*, seeing themselves in better shape than they are.

So Barry doesn't see his belly as critical to the quality of his relationship with Suzanne. Suzanne doesn't want it to be and she's well aware that it has become more of a problem to her than it is to Barry. This does not make her feel like a very nice person. Sitting on her dresser is a nasty little book called *How to Take Twenty Pounds off Your Man.* This book is based on the odious premise that the wife takes on the responsibility for her husband's weight loss, and that she dupe him for the first two weeks and not even tell him he's on the diet. All this manipulation and deception are justifiable of course because the wife can argue that *his* belly jeopardizes *her* future. She doesn't want to be without a New Year's Eve date in ten years.

Suzanne has rationalized her zealous nagging of Barry similarly. She insists it's fundamentally a health issue. It's not just a question of aesthetics. After all, she's shallow, but she's not *that* shallow. Though sometimes she wonders . . .

As does Mel. Who is into mid-life fitness as only a Californian can be and is making it very clear to his wife, Cindy, that he would like her bodily boundaries to be several sizes smaller. Like most women, Cindy has always felt overweight, but now that she's put on twenty-five pounds, Mel is seconding her opinion. She liked it better when he dissented. His remarks are making her a little nervous and a whole lot furious. Just because he is bench-pressing himself into perfection, doesn't mean he's in charge of her leg lifts too. So it becomes an issue of control. Not only weight control. But who can control the other person with the weight-control issue.

Mel doesn't think he's trying to control Cindy. But he feels entitled to tell his wife he'd find her much more attractive without the extra twenty-five pounds. If she decided to cut and dye her hair into a purple Mohawk, wouldn't he be entitled to express an opinion?

There is of course a difference between an opinion and an obsession. It seems something very ironic happens when one half of a couple gets a tad obsessed with being in condition. They get out of condition for something very fundamental to a marriage.

They get out of condition for accepting the other guy unconditionally.

You Only Get
Married for the
First Time Once

The problem with Real Life is that it really screws up BEING IN LOVE.

And since most of us have a perverse attachment to BEING IN LOVE, we tend to get all testy when Real Life starts messing up things.

Especially things like our own personal marriage. Which, of course, we all like to feel had at least something to do with BEING IN LOVE. But over the years it seems to have more and more to do with Visa bills, "I-thought-*you*-were-going-to-call-the-exterminators," and snotty comments about the truly non-fab sex that seems to be taking place on an even more truly non-fab frequency in the old communal boudoir.

Ah yes, Real Life, that incredibly whimsical little entity that invariably forces you to waken in the middle of the night, regard the slack-mouthed Significant Other sleeping next to you, and say to yourself, "Self, I might have made a serious mistake here."

Because no matter how it is, it's not "supposed to be" like this. And we're all so hung up on the "supposed to be's." Take a look at some of the things your average Fred 'n' Mabel marriage is supposed to be these days.

It's supposed to be *nurturing*.
It's supposed to be *intimate*.
It's supposed to be *challenging*.
It's supposed to be *gratifying*.

It's supposed to be *stimulating*.

It's supposed to be *romantic*.

And it's supposed to be *enlightened*. (Which just means everybody involved is responsible for his or her own orgasm.)

That's what it's "supposed to be."

And instead?

Well, for the most part it's okay. Sometimes it's even real nice. But there is indeed a fair dose of tedium, a passel of disappointments, a sprinkling of sulks, and the occasional mental flash that says, "Hey, I Definitely Deserve Better Than This."

Which, of course, you do. Sort of. Because then you have to ask yourself these two salient questions: (1) Is "better" out there? And (2) "Better" according to what? (As in "better" according to yesterday's "Oprah Winfrey Show," "better" according to this month's women's magazines, or "better" according to what Amy Farqwart down the block says her Mr. Wonderful is like?)

Nonetheless, for the most part, you tend to ignore these rumblings of domestic disgruntlement. And then one fateful day Amy and Al Farqwart—surprise, surprise—actually decide to throw in the towel. Now *that* makes you real agitated. Because it can't help but make you wonder, if Amy and Al aren't putting up with each other's shortcomings, why should you?

A very good question.

And one with an equally good answer. You should put up with each other's shortcomings because shortcomings are what it's about. Because no card-carrying grown-up walks off into the sunset just because things are slightly to the left of perfect. Which is what, dear reader, they always are.

Listen . . . you only get married for the first time once. So even though there is enormous temptation on an almost daily basis to turn to your beloved and say, "Here's your hat, there's the door," what is that going to buy you? A lot of self-righteousness and a whole bunch of evenings at Bennigan's with all the other gay divorcees, that's what.

Now don't get me wrong, it's not that I don't believe in divorce. Some of my best friends are divorced. Actually, *all* of my best friends are divorced. Divorce can be a totally right decision. It certainly is for people in pain. But I don't think it's right for people in petulance. For people who are pissed off. For people who are pouting because "supposed to be's" just aren't in place.

Listen, honey, they're never going to be in place. Think of all the things that tick you off about your lifesmate. Go on, you know what they are. You recite them several times a week at the dinner table. But have you ever noticed how they are precisely the same things that drew you to this person in the first place? For instance, there is no question but that I fell in love with my personal lifesmate because he was Marlon Brando incarnate—terribly idiosyncratic, terribly quiet, and terribly moody. Now, of course, I rail at him. Why? Because he's Marlon Brando incarnate—terribly idiosyncratic, terribly quiet, and terribly moody.

Of course there are differences. One is that at eighteen a girl always thinks that moody means "deep." At forty-four she knows it just means moody. At eighteen a girl thinks that quiet means "reflective." At forty-four she knows it usually means hostile. At eighteen a girl thinks idiosyncratic means "rugged individual." At forty-four she knows it means pain in the ass.

But she also knows it means reality. And reality cuts both ways. So she knows that he married her for her energy and enthusiasm. Which now looks a whole lot like bossiness. And he married her for her decisiveness. Which now feels a lot like adamancy. And he married her for her terrific sense of humor. Only now, quite frankly, he doesn't think she is so funny anymore. And all of it adds up to the fact that with almost no effort at all she can be quite a pain in the ass her very own self.

But the good news is that two pains in the ass can make it. They can make it when they both hold firmly to the principle that a deal is a deal. Which isn't to say that a deal has to remain a deal if it becomes untenable, but that they each signed up with the other guy knowing all those things, and that it's not particularly credible to say after fifteen or twenty years, "Sorry, darling, but I don't like the kind of human being you have been from the very beginning. I guess I just changed my mind."

Ah, *change* . . . that thorniest of notions in the old marital myth department. Because what happens when we get married is that we all are convinced we can change the other guy. And when we run up against the universally, disgustingly irrefutable fact that we can't, we are forced to acknowledge this—that the only thing that really changes in marriage is our mind, about what we'll put up with. And as we said, if you sign up with Marlon, you look just a little less than consistent if you dump him because he's Marlon.

Which brings us then to the oft-ignored virtues of hanging in there. Oft-ignored because everyone is focused instead on all those "supposed to be's."

"Supposed-to-be's" are a particularly American concept. Kind of like automatic garage-door openers. And they kind of screw you up the same way. Because you begin to perceive them as entitlements, rather than luxuries. And when for some reason they break down, as they always do, it never occurs to you to feel anything other than deprived. It never occurs to you that if you'd been willing to accept a less highfalutin concept of a garage door and/or a less highfalutin concept of a marriage, things might have been just fine, thank you.

But just fine, thank you, isn't quite enough here in the U.S. of A. Here we've got big dreams. So we computerize our garage doors and we "supposed-to-be" our marriages. Expectations run mighty tall here in the land of the free and the home of the brave. Especially when it comes to marriage. And people who live across the ocean from us, whether they live across the one to the right of us or to the left of us, seem to think we Americans are pretty silly with all our mandates for romance and personal gratification.

I know that because a few years ago I did a magazine piece called "Love and Marriage Japanese Style." And I have never forgotten when one of their foremost journalists sat me down and said, "We Japanese think all the things you Americans expect from marriage are quite ridiculous. Here in Japan, we look at marriage one way only—as a partnership in problem solving."

A partnership in problem solving. Do definitions get better than that?

Listen. In every marriage there's a moment. In every marriage there are a bunch of moments. Horrible, hurtful, I-don't-know-if-I-can-stand-one-more-minute-of-this-pain moments. But you get through them. You get through them because fundamentally your inners know there is something worth salvaging. That your tolerance may be frayed, and your goodwill somewhat eroded, and your passion may have definitely taken a sabbatical—but that in spite of all that, there is much that is worthwhile. There is history, and shared values, and a mutual delight in the miracle that two such intractable people have kept this thing together so far, and that it is well worth the effort to continue doing so. Because of one thing, because you believe fiercely in *the worthiness of the imperfect union.*

It's not considered a particularly fashionable thing to believe in these days. Not nearly as fashionable as intimacy, nurturing, et al. Witness a conversation I recently had with an old friend. She was telling me about a new book project. I asked her what it was on. It was, she said, on couples who had been together in long-term marriages. I said, Oh, you mean like old Marlon and me?

Sort of, she said. But particularly marriages in which there had been a lot of *growth.*

Growth? Oh God. Listen, when it comes to marriage, my personal feeling is that "growth" is a four-letter word.

When it comes to marriage, I believe there's a whole lot to be said for "endure."

Not for endure at any price. But for endure if at all possible. I hope it's possible for Marlon and me. Because true as it is that you only get married for the first time once, it's also true that you only get divorced for the first time once.

And I hear that one's a bitch too.

MAKING SURE THE KIDDIES HAVE ENOUGH MATERIAL FOR THEIR SHRINKS

Teenagers and the Work Ethic: A Contradiction in Terms

Now that it's summer, the topic of summer jobs becomes a particularly relevant one to explore. We shall begin by discussing the contemporary teen person vis-à-vis the historical work ethic. You remember the historical work ethic—it's the one where toil is what you do during the day, and sometimes if you're lucky you even get paid for your efforts.

Now let us discuss the contemporary teen person. That's the one who gets paid five or ten dollars a week for simply rising up every morning and continuing to breathe. You can assume that toil is not something on which the contemporary teen person has a very firm grasp. Oh, he has heard of it, and when he watched Debra Winger and Richard Gere in *An Officer and a Gentleman,* he may have even noticed that Debra had an actual factory job, but this job was pretty incidental to what the movie—and REAL LIFE—is about. Which as we all know is Sex and Falling in Love.

Unfortunately, a study was released recently that actually bolstered the argument for a teen person to avoid at all possible costs something as odious as genuine work. This study, done in Orange County, California, apparently revealed that teen persons who engage in part-time work are more likely than nonworking classmates to use marijuana and alcohol. With statistics like this, one hesitates to even imagine the consequences of full-time work.

This isn't to say that the contemporary teen person does not intend to work. He does. Later. It is, however, important to note that his concept of work hovers around something called "a career." This apparently has very little to do with "a job." A contemporary teen person can explain the difference to you. "A job" is boring. "A career" is gratifying. It also makes you rich.

This mindset is perhaps one reason for the recent *Wall Street Journal* article on the increase of geriatric burger flippers at fast food restaurants. Seems more and more teen persons are not particularly enchanted with the concept of working in a fast food emporium. In fact, to attract more teenagers, some chains are even willing to pay well over the minimum wage of $3.35. In suburban New York, where it is no doubt difficult to lure the kids off the tennis courts, some restaurants are paying as much as $5 an hour or more.

Of course the crux of the problem isn't dollars. It's that the contemporary teen person does not perceive the work ethic in terms of physical energies expended. He perceives it in terms of empire. Regaled by tales of Steven Jobs and other barely postpubescent millionaires, he knows all he need do is find Just the Right Idea. This of course is best achieved by remaining horizontal on the beach for summers on end. One wouldn't want to hamper this creative process by forcing him into any sort of menial labor such as house painting, grocery bagging, or the dispensing of fast food fried chicken parts.

Thus, the idea of summer employment becomes the moot point extraordinaire. You can't get a five-year-old to even lift up the pillow if the tooth fairy doesn't leave a minimum of a buck. Twelve years later, the kid ain't likely to mobilize his energies for a couple of bucks more. Anyway, he's busy. He's got to buff his nails for the next board of directors meeting.

The Family That Births Together

The thing I just love about "The Phil Donahue Show" is that from time to time it deposits these incredibly bizarre debates before you, on subjects you had no idea you even had an opinion on, and by 9:06 in the morning you are absolutely irate over an issue you never even knew was an issue until six minutes before. Today's issue was: Should children be permitted to witness the birth of their brother or sister?

It is quite astounding, when you think of the number of pressing quandries of contemporary life, that this thorny dilemma almost never has been among the top 10,000 questions that have haunted you. I would say it is likely that most of us have given more consideration to what we should be wearing when Paul Newman proposes to us than whether or not little Joshie should be cheering us on as we writhe and pant and blow our way through labor. Who comes up with these ideas, anyway?

Probably the same clown who decided women should have their husbands in the delivery room. Whoever came up with that one deserves to have the zipper on his or her Levis jammed for nothing less than eternity. In addition to going braless, electing Richard Nixon *twice*, and killing off the Volkswagen Beetle, encouraging a male person to pal along with you for thirty-six hours of gynecological torture was one of the worst ideas ever to come out of the sixties and seventies.

Those of us who had the misfortune to have our baby-birthing phase during those years of initial Lamaze fever would have been branded unfit, unnatural, and unchic if we had done what common sense told us to do. Which was to grunt in the privacy of your own labor room unaccompanied by a "supportive" (who got you into this, anyway?) male, take a large dose of blessedly deadening narcotics, and then wake up, when it was all over, with a little bundle of joy next to you. This was no longer allowed. Suddenly baby-having had been lifted from its rightly domain as a private, painful, rather primal act into the rather public domain where it became a participatory, practically poetic extravaganza called The (ta dum . . .) Miracle of Birth! Any man worth his salty tears on the Alan Alda Scale of Sensitivity was suddenly required to quell his gag reflex and take a front-row seat while you put on a command performance as Mother Earth. And now someone has gotten the glorious notion to change the restricted R-rating on your maternal melodrama and open it up to a PG or G audience.

Well the Donahue audience would have none of it. "No, no! A terrible idea! An absolute outrage," they railed. I seconded their sentiments, but shared none of their reasons. Reasons like: (1) A child might never recover from the vision of seeing his mother in pain. Oh, please. Every time a kid opens the cupboard and says there's nothing to eat and it's only eighteen hours after your most recent schlepp to the supermarket, a kid sees his mother in pain. Mothers are in pain all the time. Anguish is a mom's best thing. (2) A child would be bored during the long hours of labor. Well, God forbid a child of ours shouldn't be 100 percent amused at all times. (3) A child would be horrified by the sight of all that blood. Right. The same child that dragged you to see a still-beating heart ripped out of a man several summers ago in *Indiana Jones and the Temple of Doom*. He'd be just horrified.

No, the way I figure it a kid shouldn't be in the delivery room for the same reason it used to be okay to keep Dad out. The whole event still feels just a little embarrassing. You want to be real grown-up about it, but really it's such a damnably unaesthetic version of you. You're not shutting little Joshie out by not letting him in. You're just letting him "experience" one more mystery in life. Mysteries are okay. Kids do not need to know EVERYTHING.

Anyway, if they start wanting to see how their brothers and sisters are born, the next thing they'll be wanting to see is how their brothers and sisters are made. I mean, where do we draw the line, guys?

The Fear Factor

You don't know whether to label them cautious, or just crazed.

Kid #1. He is six. He walks into his parents' bedroom and solemnly sets down five copies of his school photograph, which he hates because it was taken when he was toothless. "Mom," he says, "I know you hate this picture, too, but I think you better keep it. That way, in case I get kidnapped, you'll have something to show the police."

Kid #2. He is ten and lives in a smug, upper-class suburb. Every night before he goes to bed, he sets out his arsenal. It consists of one can of Glade room freshener to spray in the anticipated assailant's eyes before unleashing his homemade weapon consisting of a six-volt battery, several straight pins set at a lethal trajectory, and a string guaranteed to ignite and incinerate his assailant. The device bears remarkable testimony to what the combination of imagination and terror can produce.

Kid #3. She is thirteen. Adult enough to cook dinners when she is baby-sitting her little sister. And adult enough to pick up the phone when Mom and Dad are at a dinner party and ask, "Hey, Mom, you know that macaroni and cheese you told me to make? The box is open so I don't think I should make it." Mom says that she is always very careful not to buy opened boxes at the store, so when she set it on the counter for dinner, she probably opened the box without thinking. The thirteen-year-old thinks it's better to throw it out. Mom say no. "Well, if we die, Mom, it's your fault."

It's always Mom's fault. We brought them into the world, the world went nuts, we wanted them to be aware of the nutsiness, and now they're nuts too. Our kids are living with a sense of imminent danger that is as acute as if they were dodging land mines in a battle-strewn war zone. The children we're raising are children of war. There is no peace when a child knows there are a lot of people out there who just can't be trusted. And sometimes they're not only strangers. Sometimes those people are even called Mom and Dad. No wonder we are raising kids who see the world as a very hostile place.

Listen, when we were young, life was not enemy-free. But the enemy was faceless, and abstract. When we crouched under our school desks in response to the nonexistent Russian bombers over-head, our hearts were not filled with terror. It was just another perfunctory school exercise. Nobody was out to get us *personally.* There were Russians and there were robbers, but we could pretty much get through months at a time without ever encountering either one of those.

But these kids have been so educated about the possible men-ace awaiting them at every level of their daily existence that they are having an increasing amount of difficulty negotiating daily exis-tence. None of us wants to see our kid so paralyzed by the potential dangers of life today that he becomes incapable of participating in life with at least some spontaneity, and at least some serenity. But how do we teach them the difference between prudence and para-noia? That too much of one is just as hazardous as too little of the other . . . ?

Kid #4. He's eight years old and four feet tall. Last week, Mom swooped into his room to give him a major battery of hugs and, because they were both standing, his face landed somewhere in the region of her less than ample breasts. The kid pushed her away, yelling, "Don't! That's child sexual abuse!"

She would have laughed—if it hadn't been so damn unfunny.

Deprived of Divorce

It's enough to give you a serious dose of the guilts. Because it's beginning to seem that if you don't get a divorce, you're doing your kid a huge disservice. Among seven studies done for a recent Institute of Mental Health report, researchers uncovered a couple of facts that almost make it sound as if divorce gives kids some major life advantages.

Academic advantages, for instance. According to one researcher, children under twelve who live with divorced mothers do better on achievement tests and have fewer school problems than kids in mom and dad homes. That's 'cause divorced moms monitor their kids more closely. (Probably because they don't have to monitor Dad anymore.)

And social advantages. Another researcher discovered that teenagers living with quarreling parents are 1.5 times more likely to lie, bully, and express antisocial behavior in general than kids with divorced parents. (Thus the longer you stay together, the greater the probability the kid will drool when taking nourishment in public places.) Additionally, it was reported that adults whose parents were divorced are arrested half as often as adults from intact homes. (Thus the longer you stay together, the greater probability the kid will wind up wearing panty hose on his face when going to cash his check at the local bank.)

Of course these are the sort of statistically quantifiable social advantages that researchers always come up with. But what about all the unquantifiable ones even you and I are smart enough to figure out? You know, the social advantages that become especially evident if your children are part of an increasing minority of kids living under the anachronistic and shameful conditions of (gasp!!!) an intact marriage.

The deprivation these children are suffering is unfathomable. First let's just speak superficially. (One of my favorite things to do.) Your heart can't help but go out to kids who have but one set of presents to open on Christmas morn. Without the old I've-got-to-outdo-my-ex-spouse competitiveness, a kid might have to settle for less than two zillion dollars' worth of merchandise.

Then let's speak culturally. Kids of divorced parents see more museums in one weekend than any intact-marriage kid sees in a year. Also, the child of divorced parents is very well traveled. No daddy wants to spend the entire spring vacation cooped up in a bachelor apartment with little people. He wants to show them a good time. Disney World in '86, dude ranch in '87, Cape Cod in '88 . . . The children of divorced parents get to see the world. Intact-marriage kids get to see their dads lying belly-up in the hammock for entire summers on end.

In addition, children of divorced couples are in better physical shape and are better all-around athletes. All those vacations provide them with the kind of skills in tennis, skiing, and scuba that an intact-marriage kid can probably only dream about.

And given the high remarriage rate for divorced people, some kids can pull in six or seven interested adults for any given back-to-school night or major basketball game. How do you think that makes a kid with a puny cheering section of two look?

Clearly, the implications of all this are profound. A child today has only a 45 percent chance of going through a parental breakup. That means less than half the children in the United States are living under optimum conditions. So if you're headed to the marriage counselor, before you decide to stay together, think twice. And for once in your life don't be selfish. Think of the children.

When Thirty
Minutes Is a Half
Hour Too Long

A study came out recently with some ostensibly gloomy statistics. Apparently most parents in America spend only about thirty minutes a day with their resident teenager. We are supposed to be a bit alarmed about this.

The statisticians noted that thirty minutes is approximately the same amount of time an adult spends watching TV news. Considering that TV news and teenagers leave the average adult feeling the same way (i.e., depressed, impotent, and furious), I do not find this surprising. The only difference is you can tune TV news out. Unfortunately this is not the case with teenagers. They tune you out first.

It happens in eighth grade. One morning the child is civil and moderately conversant—and then, *shazam!*—he goes directly into TVC (The Voice Change). Not the kind where he plummets from soprano to bass in the course of a three-letter word. But the kind of Voice Change that the girls have too. The kind they have thorough control over. Where they go from purring, giggly, tease-y inflections with other pubescent personages directly into flat, steelly, truncated tones of minimal tolerance with you. Surely no adult in his right mind can deal with this sort of disdain on a daily basis for more than three minutes max.

Another tactic teens have for making it difficult to spend extended periods of time with them is TBV (The Big Vanish). Up until twelve or thirteen years old when this child is on the premises, he feels perfectly comfortable in all of the rooms of the house, does not consider it mandatory to be the sole occupant of any one room, and has even been known to occasionally extend an invitation to another family member to join him in his own room.

Suddenly none of the above is possible. It is very difficult to have either quantity time, or even a sliver of the ever-elusive quality time, with a being who stops midsentence the minute you walk in the kitchen, and says to the person he's talking to on the phone, "Can I call you back in a little while? Someone just walked in." And it is very difficult to have quantity time, or even a sliver of the ever-elusive quality time, with someone who only emerges from his room for sustenance, a phone call, or the collection of his weekly allowance.

Another reason it is so difficult to relate for long stretches of time with a teen person is TBD (Their Basic Disapproval). Should they deign to talk to you, the majority of your conversation with them has to do with (1) how badly you behave ("Did you have to raise your hand and ask my biology teacher that question? God, I was so embarrassed!"); (2) how badly you cook ("Did you see all the preservatives on the back of this box of cereal?"); (3) how badly you dress ("Mom, you can't wear those pants—they're floods!"). Most of us cannot take that kind of contempt for anything longer than ten minutes on any given day.

And finally there is TGD (Their God-awful Disposition). Who wants to while the hours away with someone whose hormonal turbulence has them constantly lurching between giddy peaks and desolate valleys? No middle ground. Just twelve hours of *Sturm*. And twelve hours of *Drang*. Every day.

When you think about it, thirty minutes a day is not only about all any adult can take of a resident adolescent . . . it's downright masochistic.

Mom-Musings

Today I was going to talk about "Why I Like Being a Mom." I was even thinking of going a bit squishy and sentimental on you. But I'm having a lot of trouble getting in the mood. That's because I was informed a few minutes ago that a nasty little gerbil creature has escaped his cage and is running loose in the house and sorryMombutIhavetogotobaseballpractice.

This particular gerbil's name is Jackson and he is one of my least favorite things about Mom-hood. His movements are all nervous and jerky and he spends his entire day frantically spinning wheels and getting nowhere. Actually, Jackson and moms have a lot in common. Only moms never quite manage to escape.

■ ■ ■

I think I've figured out the difference between the mom of today and the mom of yesteryear. The mom of today has totally dismissed guilt-instillation as a viable tactic in dealing with her children. The modern mom does not go in for long-suffering martyrdom as our mothers did. It's too latent and subtle and muted.

We are much more overt. When a teen child calls at 5 P.M. that his Buick just broke down on the highway and he needs to get to the airport in an hour to pick up his girlfriend, and we actually drop what we are doing to fetch him from the middle of the Dan Ryan Expressway and ferret him off to O'Hare to meet his beloved, we do not greet him, as he gets into the car, with thin-lipped forbearance.

We are healthy. We are calm. We are direct. We look at that kid and we tell him the simple truth. We say, "Hey, kid. You owe me for this one."

The modern mother keeps her scoreboard out front and current at all times.

■ ■ ■

Three-thirty in the afternoon is the moment when Mom-feelings peak. If you're working, like 55 percent of the mothers in America, it is the hour you ache the most. It's the moment in the day you never quite forgive yourself for not being there. What would it be like to still feel that exquisite midday shifting of gears when you went into your "on call" mode. Where in spite of being a bit loathe to give up those last exquisite moments of domestic quiescence, you hunger to see them became noticeably acute. It was nice to savor all that lovely household serenity, but it always felt a bit vacuum-y in doses much longer than a seven-hour school day.

And as soon as they careered in, smelling of outside and mimeographed field trip notices, you were suffused with an embarrassing onslaught of love. Of course you couldn't tell them that, so you just said, "How was school?" And even though their answers were always succinct and flat (as in "Okay. What's there to eat?"), and the only further sound they made was the slamming of the refrigerator door before they ran up to their rooms, it truly didn't matter. It was an important ritual.

It is important that you're home so that you can then be ignored. It's one of the things moms do best.

Defective Parenting: An Almost Lost Art

Some kids are afflicted with a defective parent. They are the kids who have only worn sleazy, store-bought Halloween costumes. They are the kids with the slowest soapbox cars in the Cub Scouts Pinewood Derby. And they are the kids with the most burnt offerings at the Christmas bake sale. They are kids just like mine.

Defective parents are unable to make anything. We are totally devoid of small motor control, creativity, and patience. We wait with baited breath and steeled nerves for yet another event in which we will again bring humiliation down upon our children.

I have just returned from such an event. It was the Science Fair. I sent the child off to the Science Fair clutching his little shoe box full of borax, sugar, and salt crystals, totally unaware that every other child there was going to the Nobel prize in biochemistry.

I dunno. I always thought that science fairs were made up of dirt-filled Dixie Cups with little string beans growing out of them, or some sliced-off Ping-Pong balls glued to a cardboard and called "Our Solar System," or a box lined with cotton batting featuring some poor pinioned butterflies.

Fade to Science Fair '88. Where video has arrived. Where a twenty-inch TV screen featured a continuous video of the step-by-step process little Jason went through in order to put together his display titled "How Neon Works." "How Neon Works" was filled with luminous tubes, color photographs of Jason working with the tubes, and the kind of technical explanations usually reserved for footnotes in *Science Digest*. It was the ultimate in show-biz science —something of a cross between PBS and MTV.

Moving right along to the living-creature division . . . in a stunning exhibition worthy of alienating any animal husbandry advocates, little Pearson displayed two little guinea pigs. One was plump and perky and the other was cadaverous and clearly on the verge of stepping into another guinea pig time zone. The cataclysmic difference in their appearances was due to the diet Pearson had been shoving down them for three months. The perky, porky one had been eating judiciously balanced meals from the seven basic food groups. But the emaciated one had been guinea-pigging out on junk food—soda, nachos, and Twinkies. It was a dazzling, if less than humane, display. And certainly a provocative one—considering that this was scientific proof you can lose more weight on Twinkies than on salad.

Then we strolled down volcano row. Where several dads must have spent hundreds of hours frolicking with chicken wire, papier-mâché, and paint. Not to mention dealing with the joys of bubbling dry ice. These were followed by the functioning boat lock that worked with valves, pulleys, and real water, or the gen-u-ine dam with gen-u-ine waterwheel, gen-u-ine water, and gen-u-ine irrigation ditches. We also saw a gen-u-ine week-old baby, which, given the rather realistic displays, made us momentarily concerned that some kid was going for the gold in a reproduction experiment. However, it only turned out to be someone's little sister.

At the end of the Science Fair, my kid put his crystals in his shoe box, and sighed with great resignation. "Don't feel bad, Mom. Guess what the science teacher told me? He patted me on the head and said, 'If it weren't for kids like you, the Japanese might really have something to worry about.'

"What's that mean, Mom?"

Beatlesharing

Most of us are always crabbing about how it's so much harder to be a parent today. Harder than when we grew up. And in lots of ways it is.

When we grew up parents could send a kid off to the store for a loaf of bread and be fairly certain the kid would return.

And when we grew up, parents might notice the kid had a runny nose, but their big worry was that the kid had a cold—not a cocaine problem.

And when we grew up, "sexually active" was not an option for "nice" girls. So the only pill our parents worried we might forget to take was our vitamin pill.

So in many ways it is harder now. It's certainly more complicated. But there is one small, lovely way in which it is definitely easier to be a parent today.

The music. Remember when our folks listened to Sinatra and we listened to Elvis, and it seemed that never the twain would meet? Well it has. It's met right here in the scary, complex, topsy-turvy 1980s. We may still battle with our kids over messy rooms, and curfews, and telephone privileges, but, miracle of miracles, when they get in the car, most of the time it is possible for us to actually listen to the same radio station.

Granted, this is not true for the Montovani moms and Adam Ant adolescents. But for many of us who fall somewhere in the middle of the musical spectrum, it's just as likely that Mom will be listening to The Eagles as it is for her daughter to be listening to The Eagles. Or to Springsteen. Or to Phil Collins.

No longer is there a mandatory chasm between "our" music and "their" music like when we were young. Remember how resistant Mom and Dad were to all of it? Not just to Elvis, but to Little Richard and to Bill Haley and even to the Beatles. Most of them just hated the stuff. And they were convinced that it was just a momentary musical aberration.

Of course rock and roll never did die, it just kept on evolving along. And one of the most gratifying results of that is that today's kids actually have a lot of affection—I'd even go so far as to say respect—for some of that earlier music—"our" music.

Not that they always realize it's "our music." Last year we were in the car when my daughter started singing along to "Sea of Love" by the Honeydrippers. The record had only been out a few days so she was somewhat stunned when old Mom jumped in and knew every last word. Of course I'd committed it to memory years ago when Phil Phillips recorded it in 1959.

Interestingly, in the past few years there have been a lot of those rehabbed rock hits that span the mother-daughter bridge. Her David Lee Roth recorded my Beach Boys' "California Girls." Her Mick Jagger and David Bowie recorded my Martha and the Vandellas' "Dancin' in the Street." And our Phil Collins recorded the Supremes' "You Can't Hurry Love."

I'm not saying that all of this means a whole lot in the greater scheme of things. But loving and listening to the same music as your kids is a somewhat unique and comforting aspect of parenting today.

At least this way you both can sing along to the same song while you're driving him back to reform school.

The Call You Shouldn't Make

*S*he knew she would regret it.

Each time she did it, she swore she never would again. And yet it was this terrible, intense compulsion. For five minutes she fought valiantly against this driving need within her. But she just couldn't help herself . . .

You have just read:

   a. The start of a B-level romance novel.

   b. The description of a person with a serious drug or chocolate addiction.

   c. The feelings every working mother has before she picks up the phone and calls home . . . just to check in.

Every time we do it, we get more than we bargained for. It is always The Call We Know We Shouldn't Make.

Walk along the corridors of any airport where every wall phone has a human being glued to it, and listen. The men are all calling their offices. The women are all calling home. For one last check.

For instance. It is 8 A.M. at O'Hare. You left your home exactly forty-five minutes before. One urchin was safely off to summer school. The other was to be picked up for summer camp at eight-thirty. He had wished you a groggy good-bye and had three alarm clocks flanking his pillow. Unless he had suddenly gone brain dead, he couldn't have avoided hearing them when they went off.

But you of course felt compelled to Be Sure. To Check In. To Touch Base. God forbid you should just assume he had gotten up, gulped a bowl of cereal, and gotten off to camp. God forbid. So you consider calling. You know you shouldn't. But every phone you pass beckons to you. Every quarter in your wallet mocks you. You call. And what do you get?

Exactly what you deserve. Major aggravation.

You get a smart-mouthed kid with about four hundred reasons why he shouldn't go to camp that day, but instead should stay home unsupervised and watch rented movies with two of his friends. By the time you hang up, large chunks of energy that you had planned to use for navigating in New York City had been depleted by an eleven-year-old in the Chicago suburbs.

Of course you do have a soulmate right next to you. Another working mom sets down her briefcase, plunks in her quarter, and makes The Call You Know You Shouldn't Make. "Hi, Mrs. Brown, is everything okay . . . ? Oh no. She does . . . ? How high is it . . . ? Is she crying like something hurts her . . . ? Did you call the doctor? You mean he can't see her sooner . . . ? Okay . . . No, I'm not worried . . . I'll call back just as soon as I land in Minneapolis."

Why do we do this? Why do we feel driven to call when the last time we left the premises everything was A-OK? You know why.

We do this for the same reason we call every day at three-fifteen.

So if they're not home at three o'clock, we can have the pleasure of going insane.

We do this for the same reason we sleep on the floor of their room when they are really sick.

So we don't miss a moan.

Dollars and Kid Sense

It is frequently said that children do not know the value of money. This is only partially true. They do not know the value of *your* money. *Their* money, they know the value of.

Let me explain how this works. You will note that when the average American child sees something he wants, whether it's a pair of $50 red high tops or a $79.95 remote control Destructo laser spacecraft, he hesitates not a minute to ask you for it. You of course say no and then tell him something nice and original like money doesn't grow on trees. He says he knows, that it comes from the twenty-four hour teller window at the bank from which he has seen you extract fistfuls of twenties in the middle of the night. You say, yeah, but I work hard for my money. And he says what's the point of working for money if you're never going to spend it.

It is interesting then to watch as the child grows up how he revises his views about money. This isn't to say he doesn't still expect to be paid a handsome allowance simply for waking up every morning and continuing to blink. But his attitude does change.

For example, suppose there is in your household a teenager who, for the first time in her short but catered-to life, actually worked a forty-hour week for the entire summer. It was not a glamorous career-girl-in-training sort of position in which she got to carry a briefcase or wear smart little suits. She worked in a warehouse. And it was hot and gritty and real exhausting. For her efforts she was paid minimum wages. But she never called in sick and she lasted all twelve weeks. You, in fact, were pleased to note that the kid, who had displayed occasional princess leanings, really hung in there.

There was one reason for that—she loved her paycheck. Not *"loved"*—but LOVED. She looked at that paycheck and major passion for each and every penny surged through her avaricious little body. By the end of summer, given a choice between dinner with Tom Cruise and an actual cash bonus, the child would most definitely have put her bankbook above her hormones.

Thus, last week, when the child asks if she can go to New York for a visit, you say fine, if she will split the cost of her airfare. The child is *totally appalled* by this suggestion. You can't believe it. New York is her favorite place in the world. You ask her if it isn't worth a hundred dollars to go to New York. She says of course it's worth a hundred dollars. One hundred of *your* dollars. Not of hers.

What you forgot was this. Her money, earned by her sweat, is sacrosanct. Yours is to be spent. Her money is to be cherished. Yours is to be spent. Her money is to remain intact. Yours is to be spent.

Ultimately you convince her that the only way she will see the Big Apple is to make a 50-percent contribution to the plane ticket fund. It is with great reluctance then that she goes into the bank. You would have thought in fact that asking her to withdraw one hundred dollars of *her money* was tantamount to asking her to amputate a leg or something.

She, however, does exit with one hundred of her hard-earned smackeroos. And a slight limp.

The Joys of
Junior High

On the old pain-o-meter, Sandra is logging in some pretty impressive numbers. Because the hurt is horrendous—once again she's got a kid enduring the social savagery of junior high. Good old junior high—the place that makes the nine circles of Dante's hell seem like a Club Med.

Of course this time Sandra is getting the more primitive version of junior high torment. This time she's got a boy going through it. So the hazing and the hurts are more direct and forthright. Instead of the subtle, ice-cold cruelties that seventh-grade girls can inflict on each other, the format this time is very simple: They just beat the living daylights out of each other. On the bus, in the halls, in the locker room, no matter. Every day for three weeks now, her kid comes in and tells her about this ninth-grade bully who just clobbers him.

So once again Sandra gets to experience the same swell set of emotions she got to deal with a few years ago when her daughter was the victim-of-the-month of this regulation adolescent torment. Once again Sandra gets to experience rage at the injustice. And impotence to do much about it.

Because the fundamental rule still applies: NO MATERNAL INTERVENTION. No matter that her kid doesn't stand a chance, since the ninth grader is two years older and thirty pounds heavier than her kid. No matter that she happens to be semi-friends

with the mom of the kid who is pummeling her son. No matter
. . . she is not permitted to say a word.

Especially since her husband is Type 2. There are two kinds of
dads on this stuff. Type 1 dads go insane when they hear their kid is
being pulverized, and they have to be physically restrained from
going over to the bully's house and threatening to beat the kid's
brains out. Type 2 dads are precisely 180 degrees removed from
that. It's not that they don't care, but they look at this as a fundamental male rite of passage. They figure that the kid has two
choices—either to walk away, or to learn how to defend himself.
Sort of a "Whaddya want to be kid—Martin Luther King or
Chuck Norris?" Or course trying to be Martin Luther King doesn't
really cut it in a junior high's *Lord of the Flies* environment, and
trying to be Chuck Norris will probably get the kid killed.

Still, Sandra hopes her son tries the latter. She figures at least
if there is an actual bloodletting, then she can legitimately inter-
vene and call the bully's mom. She almost laughs at the perversity
of this modern-day biblical situation, realizing that apparently
Abraham wasn't the only one willing to go in for some serious
sacrificing. On the other hand, she can't see any other way out.

And at least this time there *might* be a way out. A phone call
following an actual physical injury is definitely a way to actively *do*
something. When her daughter was in junior high five years ago,
and was ostracized on the bus and in the lunchroom, Sandra
watched helplessly while the icy silence and vicious slurs almost
destroyed the child. It was the worst experience she can remember
as a parent. This time she has to admit that the pain is more
endurable.

Somehow it's easier to deal with a broken nose than a broken
heart.

Back to School—
Thank God

Kids wait for Christmas. Moms wait for today. Today is back-to-school day. Today is December 25 for a large portion of the adult populace. Today is the day you never, ever, thought would finally come.

Today is the day you can reassert your territoriality. The joint becomes yours again from eight-thirty until three-thirty. For seven wondrous hours. You walk around the edges of the place like a cat. You mutter under your breath, "Mine, mine, mine." You can hardly believe *they're* gone.

The phone is yours again. The kitchen is yours again. The bathroom is yours again. Even if you're off at the office, you feel serenity is yours again just knowing the place isn't being defiled while you're gone for nine straight hours—now it will only be defiled for two. This you can deal with. Almost gracefully.

Today is the day you stop hearing the word "boring." This has been the most frequently uttered word of the past three months. This word has filled in the blank in the following sentences:

The beach is _____.
The pool is _____.
Baseball is _____.
Tennis is _____.
My bike is _____.
Reading is _____.

All my friends are _____.

It's your fault that everything is _____.

Today is the day you wake up at dawn to pack the most artful, wholesome, well-balanced little lunches of the year. All seven food groups are actually represented. Of course, *you* know, and the kid knows, that this frenzied attempt at *haute* nutrition lasts about seventy-two hours and then after that it's pbj's on the least moldiest slices of bread available. But today you even cut off the crust. Nice touch.

Today is the day you start counting from. "What do you mean you need new jeans? When school started I bought you three new pairs." Same with tennis shoes and same with lunch boxes. None of the above will last an entire year. They always die in February. Except lunch boxes. They wait until April to die. Locating a Smurf lunch box in April is akin to stumbling across the Holy Grail in a K mart parking lot. It is not going to happen.

Today is the day it begins all over. The car pools, the nagging to make sure they've done their homework, the discipline conferences with the teachers, the last-minute rush to the library because the Helen Keller paper is due in three days, the suspension notice from the hockey team . . . all the stuff you love to crab about, but find infinitely more enjoyable than what you've been through for the last three months. Today they're finally back in school. Where they belong.

Yes, Virginia, there really is a Santa Claus.

Every Day Is Grown-Up Day

Somewhere between Mother's Day and today most of us have been asked the following question by the resident short people in the family: "Why isn't there a Children's Day?"

And then we tell them what our parents always told us: "Every day is Children's Day." Which, if you think about it, is really a bunch of bull.

It's horrible being a kid. But we haven't been a kid for so long that we tend to glamorize it. It's the old grass is greener concept. We look at kid-dom and think of it as catching fireflies, and being in school plays, and finding red bikes under Christmas trees. Even in today's world, where eight-year-olds are taking courses in stress management, we still look at kid-dom as a marvelous exemption from grown-up drudgery like balancing checkbooks, and taking the car in, and sewing on name tags, and worring about job security, and cleaning out the refrigerator.

And that's true. Except I'd rather be a grown-up than a kid any day. And it has nothing to do with being wiser, more experienced, and more enriched. It has to do with more important things.

The most important one is that when you are a grown-up you get to eat anything you want. No one makes a grown-up eat his lima beans. When you are a grown-up you can eat lox and cream cheese, pretzels, and Raisinets for dinner and there's not a soul in the world who can stop you. You can order a pizza at unspeakable hours. You don't have to clean your plate in order to have your chocolate pudding. And you never, never have to finish your crusts.

When you are a grown-up you get to go to bed when you want. *(When* you want, not always *with whom* you want.) No lights out at ten-thirty so you always have to miss half of "L.A. Law." No humiliating negotiating on weekends for an extra hour instead of a half hour because Mr. T. is on Saturday Night Live this week. It's just you, the alarm clock, and your innate high standards for television viewing.

When you are a grown-up your mother can't yell at you anymore. This doesn't mean you are exempt from her wrath. You are never exempt from her wrath. But once you are a grown-up she can't yell at you about your clothes, your friends, the way you keep your room. The best she can do is get off a few venomous zingers. And sigh a lot. Her arsenal is seriously diminished.

When you are a grown-up you don't have to study for geometry tests. Tell the truth, is there a day that goes by when you don't breathe a sigh of relief that you are exempt forever from isosceles triangles? That you'll never again be obliged to know the terms of the treaty following the Franco-Prussian War? And that unless you move to Paris, you'll probably never have to worry how to say in French, "I wouldn't have gone there if I hadn't had to."

It's definitely better to be a grown-up than a kid. Except when it comes to soothing your nerves. Just think of the fortune you could save on Valium if sucking your thumb would do the trick again.

Mesopotamia Strikes Again

All summer long, mothers across America mutter, "God, I cannot wait until school starts." Mothers mutter this because they have apparently forgotten some of the more distressing aspects of having a child back in school. Aspects like complex car-pool schedules. Or having to nag the kid about his math assignment. And most heinous and terrifying of all . . . term papers.

Term papers have always been terrifying, but it used to be only the students who were terrified. Now it's Mom and Dad, too. As I recall most of our parents were totally oblivious to the fact that we were immersed in a serious fifth-grade report on the everyday life of the earthworm. We might have told them, but their only involvement would be to say, "That's nice, dear."

Fade to the eighties. It's "Parents Night" in the seventh-grade ancient civilizations class. A teacher, who looks like he has been around since most of the world's ancient civilizations, proceeds to explain the semester's curriculum. All is going swimmingly until he announces, "And there will be one term paper."

The collective color in the collective cheeks of the collective parents collectively drains. Eyes frantically dart about in the hopes that some other parent will have the nerve to ask the big question that has frozen everybody's heart. A senior vice-president of a major ad agency begins to sweat blood. Timidly, he raises his hand and croaks, "How long a paper, Mr. Farqwart?"

Mr. Farqwart has been at this a very long time. With masterful cruelty he says, "As long as it takes to cover the subject."

Throats tighten. So he's going to play that way, is he? Another brave soul ventures forth, "Um, Mr. Farqwart, are you going to require footnotes?"

Disdain drips from his answer. "Well this IS the seventh grade . . ."

Tremulously, another full-grown adult inquires, "How big a part of their grade is this going to be, Mr. Farqwart?"

"Half," he says. Twenty grown-ups leave that room considerably less happy than when they walked in.

It is only a matter of weeks then till the seventh grader comes home and says, "Mr. Farqwart assigned us a term paper on Mesopotamia." What this translates to in practical terms is akin to a gun going off and starting gates being opened at the Preakness. Twenty sets of parents charge to their cars, and careen to their libraries, and by seven that evening every available book on Mesopotamia has been sucked out of the entire city and suburban library system.

Then every night for the next four or five weeks it's serious business. When you're not hounding them to work on their note cards, you're helping them proofread the fourteenth version of their bibliography. The thing is, you keep saying to yourself, "Wait a minute. I already did seventh grade. I've already been terrorized by the Mr. Farqwarts of the world. I've already had to memorize the difference between Assyria and Babylonia. I've already put in my time discussing the development of cuneiform writing." At least that's what you plan to say . . .

Just as soon as you finish looking up whether there is one *m* or two *m*'s in Code of Hammurabi . . .

Soap and Swears

When I was a kid in the Pleistocene Age, about the worst, most ominous, most terror-instilling item in the household was . . . the dreaded bar of Lava soap. That industrial-strength, gritty, dark gray rectangle used to sit menacingly on the kitchen sink and absolutely radiate intimidation.

It was nasty enough having to use that gritty, evil-smelling soap on our grubby little kiddie hands before being permitted re-entry into our supersanitized households. But the real horror, and the real panic, came from Lava's other widespread household application—washing out young, surly, swear-spewing mouths.

It always seemed that within two minutes of having uttered the d-word or the h-word, an adult you were related to magically appeared on the scene to drag you off for the dreaded soaping. One noxious cleansing and it was months before you even risked a "darn" or "heck."

Fade to the eighties, when d-words and h-words are really the least of it. Rolling off the tongue of any contemporary six-year-old are words that you didn't even *know* existed until you were well into your twenties. And what makes it so surrealistic is that said six-year-old will sally forth these profanities with such a chilling absence of relish. And with minimal comprehension of what he is actually saying. At least when we said the d-word or the h-word, we knew we had said something heinous and despicable and deliciously BAD. But the even the s-word and the f-word and all those other words are so flattened out today and so empty that the kids don't even think of them as foul.

I say that because yesterday I was asked the following question by a child of single-digit years. (Actually, due to the constraints of my inherent good taste, I am unable to relay the question in its entirety. But you'll get the missing part of the question if you just think about Dick and Jane. And then forget about one of them. The question was, "Hey, Mom. How come there isn't any swear word for d——?"

When I pulled myself up off the linoleum, I tried valiantly to convince the child that "d——" was indeed as sweary a swear word as is currently available in the linguistic marketplace. My efforts were to no avail. He was adamant that it was perfectly acceptable medical terminology or an interchangeably innocuous substitute for the word "jerk." It became clear that some serious measures were necessary.

I bought some Lava soap. I explained to the child about Lava's searing potency, its brute force, its fearsome heavy-duty efficacy. And then I unwrapped the fearsome weapon . . . What?? The Lava of the eighties was smooth, delicately perfumed, and a pale, lovely shade of green. Where was the killer abrasion, the dark foreboding gray, the terrifying promise of torture?

Thanks a lot, Proctor & Gamble. What kind of pansy soap is that? Now you're forcing me to take even more drastic measures than my parents took. I really had hoped to avoid this, but you're forcing me to go for the ultimate solution.

The one where I have to stop swearing too.

Life in the Popular Lane

How do you convince a teen person that there really will be a day when being "popular" or "unpopular" will no longer be the all-consuming, all-encompassing, consummate criteria of her every waking moment? That one day it will cease being the pivotal issue it is during adolescence and will be reduced to . . . an insidiuously subliminal issue? Surely one of the more sensational aspects about being a card-carrying grown-up is that though "popular" never really vanishes, at least it is finally forced into the closet.

The kid will never believe it won't always be a life-and-death issue. Not when she feels irrevocably branded and chained to some spot on the mid to lower level of a very precise pyramid of popularity, where rankings *seem* as blatant and definitive as if they were the final standings of the Miss America Pageant being etched in stone for eternity.

Seem is the operative word here. Because there is a very interesting quirk about "popular." Hardly anyone, not even the ostensibly "popular," ever really feels "popular." My friend Sally of the strawberry-blonde hair, Betty Boop blue eyes, and unmatchable pom-pom-girl talents had an undisputable crème de la crème ranking for four entire years. Ask anyone from Beverly Hills High School's Class of '61. Except Sally. Who will tell you with a surplus of incredulity that she can't believe anyone ever considered her a major wheel. And who recalls only that, even though she happened to be best friends with the homecoming queen, she ached with

despair over not being accepted into the class's clique of sophisticates. Sally, who has about thirty-seven pictures in the senior year-
book (we're talking class secretary, student council pictures, not
science club or cafeteria council pictures), has not one recollection
of ever really feeling securely ensconced near the pinnacle of the
pyramid. That's what a wonderfully reassuring principle "popular"
is.

With the exception of a belly button, there's probably no
more universal scar than the one left by this damnable, dopey pre-
cept of "popular." You don't have to have been Janis Joplin to feel
permanently stigmatized by those years of feeling thoroughly unacceptable. And though there are a slew of singer, writer, show-biz
types who have converted their devastation into creative I'll-Show-
Them careers, most rank and file folk have to acquire their vindica-
tion by considerably more prosaic methods.

My friend Elaine's fifteen-year-old daughter, Susan, is adamant that nothing short of a $1,500 nose job can give her a fighting
chance at "popular." She does not want to hear one more Barbra
Streisand or Bette Midler ugly-duckling-makes-good story. She's fifteen. As far as Susan's concerned, she IS her nose. She doesn't want
to wait and I'll-Show-Them her way through life. She wants to be
one of Them. Now.

Elaine wants to tell Susan that even with a new nose it's possible that she won't become "popular." But she hopes that won't be
true. Elaine wants to tell Susan that in real life "popular" doesn't
matter. But she knows that isn't true. She used to think it was. She
used to think that just because adults never describe people as "the
most popular couple on the block" or "the most popular account
executive in the office," the tyranny of "popular" had finally been
vanquished. But over the years she has seen that that isn't the case.

"Popular" simply goes underground. It becomes too embarrassing to admit that it still matters. It matters a little less crucially,
but you know it still matters when you and your husband are one of
three couples on the block not invited to the Christmas party of
some neighbors down the street. Or you know it matters when
you've recently been divorced and your good friend calls another
woman you know to fix her up with the attractive new lawyer who
just moved to town. Or you know it matters when everyone in the

office goes off for drinks on Friday night and somehow you weren't asked to go along again. You're not supposed to care about those things the way you did when you were sixteen. So you just wince instead of crumble.

But it still smarts. I just barely missed smarting last weekend. My college sorority was throwing a twentieth reunion, and the big feature was that we were all sleeping at the house on campus. There we were, thirty-two 40-year-old women who had written movies, become physicians, performed on Broadway, founded our own businesses, and raised a total of seventy-three children—all of us scrambling around the room saying, "Do you want to room together?" with the panic of a new camper who has three seconds left to clamp onto a partner for the buddy system. I couldn't believe it. I have authored one book, write a nationally syndicated column, speak two foreign languages, have two rather sterling offspring, of whom I am terrifically proud, and I wouldn't have felt worth a damn if my friend Ellen hadn't asked me to room with her.

So I lack a bit of credibilty when I spend an average of forty-seven minutes a week giving impassioned speeches to my resident adolescent that just because the phone hasn't rung for three straight days doesn't mean she isn't a perfectly swell human being. I have this great line about how swell really is a relative state of being and that for sure there are plenty of people in our lives who will probably think we are unswell. Which 1) doesn't mean we are; 2) is something we can live with. I don't mention 3): You still wish like crazy they thought you were swell.

I wish it weren't true, but the clout of "popular" is relentless. In fact there's only one thing tougher to satisfy than our endless desire to be liked by bunches of people. And that's our endless desire to be loved by one.

Remote-ing Your Control

I just read an article that has to be 100 percent wrong. It says that the remote control device on our TVs is the hot, new arena for family conflict. The theory is that whoever controls the device, controls the household, and that people are always seeking more control of the household.

Wrong-o. Most of us are seeking precisely the opposite—less control of a household. Most of us already have more control than we know what to do with. And we'd be real thrilled to unload it all. For instance, take a look at this partial list of the things most modern women can claim total control of in the average American household.

The absence, presence, and folded-ness of clean clothes for all family members. For years, we have been seeking to abandon control of this challenging domain, but to no avail. Is there any moment more bloodcurdling in the annals of relationship-having than this one: "Honey, where are my brown argyle socks?" Only the moment that follows—the one when we realize that we actually do know the precise whereabouts of the brown argyle socks.

The absence, presence, and cooked-ness of all foods for all family members. Thus even if the old man has taken the day off and is hungry around dinnertime, it is still the little woman who remains in complete control of orchestrating and serving his dinner.

Additionally, most of us can claim complete control over whether or not the houseplants die of thirst, whether or not all mothers-in-law receive Christmas presents, and whether or not the children ever put in a personal appearance at the dentist. So you see, many of us feel we already have more control than we bargained for.

Thus it is hard to envision the modern woman rushing into the TV room to wrest the remote control device out of the hands of a family member. In our house, for instance, we have had one of these devices for a year and I still do not know how to operate it. Just as I do not know, or want to know, how to operate the videocassette recorder. There is something enormously attractive about remaining purposefully obtuse in this department, because as long as I remain totally inept, someone else gets to be in charge. It ain't much, but it is a swell little moment in my personal life when I turn to the resident eleven-year-old and say, "Set up the tape for 'Moonlighting,' honey. You know Mommy can't figure that thing out yet." Ignorance may not be bliss, but it definitely offers some respite, some distance, and a certain momentary removal from responsibility.

And that's all any woman really wants. What we long for has a lot less to do with control than it has to do with remote.

Whip Me, Whip Me . . .

You've asked yourself a trillion times: HOW DID THIS HAPPEN?

And you keep coming up with the same truly unsatisfactory answer: BECAUSE YOU LET IT HAPPEN, DORKHEAD.

Can this be? Can it be that a woman who almost had her life in perfect order, who almost had her life in the kind of shape a modern gal can only dream of, can it be that this woman voluntarily takes that practically perfect life and makes sure that it is accessorized with a steaming pile of caa-caa?

Literally. Because you just acquired a puppy. ("Puppy" being something of a euphemism for what you actually acquired—which is a seventy-five pound Doberman.) This seventy-five-pound bundle of slobbering joy comes to you courtesy of a twelve-year-old boy who has started every sentence in the past week like this: "Mom, can't we just try her? Otherwise they may have to take her to the pound." Then the blue eyes tear up a lot, which is a pretty cheap trick considering the family already has a seventy-five-pound German shepherd who is dear and well-trained and totally fulfills all your personal requirements for canine companionship. So you say NO, thereby being made to feel that you are a person in the same category of compassion and warmth as perhaps Rasputin and Goebbels.

All this is going on at the precise moment when your life as a working mom is about to become nothing short of, as we said, perfect. ("Perfect" being a euphemism for no kids and no husband.) Overnight camp beckons one, a two-week visit with granny beckons the other, and even Mr. Wonderful has to be out of town for two weeks on biz. What you've got there, girl, is nothing short of domestic nirvana—no marketing, no bickering, no ironing, and no rock and roll after midnight. You are at long last going to be able to reach for your razor and find it in the exact same place you left it. ("Exact same place" being a euphemism for your actual bathroom.) In any case, you are about to have everything you always dreamed of—a two-week slice of solitude right in your own backyard.

Only you make sure that it never happens. Because right there in your own backyard is something very different from solitude. Right there in your own backyard is a maniac of a Doberman—wreaking havoc with your lawn, wreaking havoc with your logic, and wreaking havoc with your life.

Because you caved in. You took that two weeks of perfection and completely trashed it. You finally said YES to the dog. And that, dear girl, is precisely HOW it happened.

WHY it happened is something else. But it's something you have finally figured out. You let the dog in because your life was about to be perfect. And the truth is, perfection is a woman's enemy. The truth is, a woman *needs* something to crab about. Without something to crab about, how else does a woman know she's alive?

The truth is, Descartes was only partially right. What he really meant to say was, "I bitch, therefore I am."

The Barbie Battle

It's not that Jessica Lange is a liar.

Everyone knows what a pillar of principle the woman is. So I think she truly *believes* that she will actually accomplish this.

But she'll never pull it off. No way. Because millions of women before her have tried. And failed miserably. Millions of women have said the very same thing that Jessica Lange said in this month's *Esquire*. Millions of women have said, "I'm never going to let my daughter have a Barbie."

And then one day they had a daughter in the house.

And then one day they had a Barbie in the house. Not only did they have a Barbie, but they had Barbie Hot Tubs, Barbie campers, Barbie Workout Centers, zillions of Barbie glitter clothes, and most heinous of all, tens and tens of pairs of those microscopic slingback Barbie-shoes that are always derailing from those stunted little Barbie-feet, getting hopelessly lost, and triggering vats of tears from Barbie-owners.

This, however, is not a piece in which we will launch into the usual litany of Barbie-abominations. By now, everything that can be said has been said about this eleven-and-one-half-inch idolette who has no life apart from her clothes and her car. Whose freakishly perky breasts, and horrifically choked waist, and lavishly fat hair have distorted little girls corporal expectations for a quarter of a century.

What this is about is the folly, the arrogance, and the futility of a statement like Jessica Lange's.

Oh, Jessica. Let me tell you something. We know it requires great fortitude to defy convention and have two children out of wedlock. And we know it requires great conviction to march into the U.S. Congress and badger them about the plight of the farmer. But that is nothing—I repeat *nothing*—compared to the conviction and fortitude you are going to need in order to keep Barbie out of your daughter's life.

Listen, you think you have it all under control. But, Jessica, your daughter Shura is only four years old. Wait. Wait until she becomes socialized. Wait until it becomes apparent she is the only kid in the first or second grade whose mommy won't let her have a Barbie. And the pressure is really on. And when there is a Barbie sleepover party at little Mindy's house. And Shura isn't invited. Because she doesn't have a Barbie. And there's nothing between her and this party but your politics. How long are you going to be able to last?

Listen, Jessica. You don't think the millions of American women who purchased the nearly quarter of a billion Barbies sold over the years didn't make this speech, too? We all have succumbed. Better women than I have succumbed. And dare I say it, it's possible even better women than you have succumbed. In fact, I once heard a rumor, but it was only hearsay, that Vanessa Vadim (daughter of you-know-who Fonda) once even had a Fashion Photo Barbie. Now if that's true, what kind of chance do you think you have?

Because we crumble. We all start out with smug little speeches just like yours and, whether it's a Barbie or a GI Joe or Rainbow Bright, ultimately we all cave in. I guarantee you, Jessica, that four years from now, you are not going to want to be reminded of that speech.

Remember one thing, Jessica . . . the road to Toys "Я" Us is paved with good intentions.

BOOGYING WITH THE DAILY INSANITIES

The Old Homestead Ain't What It Used to Be

Dear Thomas Wolfe:

You were right. You *can't* go home again. Especially when your home was in Beverly Hills. And your once modest (by B.H. standards, anyway) neighborhood has suddenly gotten chi-chi-fied into a very glitzy zone. And your old no-name next-door neighbors have now been replaced by the likes of Bette Midler and Brandon Tartikoff. I tell you, Tom, it's pretty weird, pretty weird.

Of course you can't help knocking on the front door anyway. Because even though you haven't set foot in the place for twenty-five years, this is still the edifice that makes bimonthly appearances in all your primal dreams. You know how it is, Tom; the house you grew up in lives in a permanent time warp dead center in the old dream gland. Which is why there just aren't a whole lot of us who can resist ringing that doorbell and checking the place out again.

So a guy answers. And you explain your whole dopey story. And of course he gets it instantaneously because, after all, he grew up in another house three thousand miles to the east and he's always wondered what it was like, too. So you cross the threshold. And in that one moment you change forever the landscape of those dreams.

Because "different" doesn't even begin to say it. It's almost as if it were defiantly different. It's almost as if someone came in and said, Now what can I do to this joint so when the previous owners come over someday they will go directly into cardiac arrest? Because the entire place has done a real 180. Your house was tailored and tan. This house is frilly and floral. Your house was open and kind of spare. This house is cozy and kind of busy. We are definitely talking altered states.

We are talking family room that has become a dining room. And dining room that has become a living room. And weirdest of all, wildest of all, worst of all we are talking little girl's bedroom that has become a library! Tom, it was unnerving enough standing in the space that used to be a dining room and realizing that it was right here, right here within these four walls, at those cacophonous family dinners, that every neurotic component of your being was instilled.

But that was nothing, nothing to stepping inside your very own pink-and-white/destined-to-be-a-princess bedroom and finding it metamorphosed into an extremely serious library. The walls you once lined with Ricky Nelson photos are now covered with leather-bound books. The TV corner where for years you watched the torrid romance of Kenny and Arlene on "American Bandstand" is now filled with a collection of antique English paperweights. And the bed on which you wept buckets because Joey didn't call is now replaced by stacks and stacks of theater memorabilia. You look at that room and you'd never even have an inkling that there was rock 'n' roll in them thar walls.

Yup, Tom, as you predicted, it's real hard to be cool about this. So it's no surprise that little tears well up in the old mid-life eyes. It is the strangest sort of estrangement. It is the most rapacious sort of rape. It is the most invasive sort of invasion. I tell you, Tom. It's as if . . . as if . . .

It's as if someone else actually lived there.

The Well-Dressed Icebox

It's impossible to break the icebox habit.

Not the habit where you can't stop calling it an "icebox." And not the habit where you can't stop raiding the thing you still call an "icebox." I'm talking about the habit where you can't stop affixing little clippings and cleverisms to the door of this thing you still call an "icebox."

Of course there are those who would say if God had intended for icebox doors to be naked he would not have invented little magnets in the shape of broccoli. This is a difficult metaphysical point to dispute. I personally cannot fathom a finer place to showcase a tasteful diagram of the Heimlich maneuver or a panic-instilling list of the Top 73 Household Poisons than on the front of the fridge. Drawers devour items like that and you'd never locate them in the nick of time.

So fridge-littering, while perhaps a bit unaesthetic to those seeking a high-tech look, does have its defensible points. Nonetheless, when my fifteen-year-old fridge died a sudden but noble death a few weeks ago, I vowed that the spiffy new replacement I'd just spent major bucks on would remain sleek and pristine. That my $801 state-of-the-art icebox would not metamorphose into a large rectangle shaggily festooned in yellowing newsprint.

And for the first few days, I stuck to my promise. But it was not easy. It was not easy to walk into the kitchen and see nothing but a huge white impersonal hunk of unadorned refrigeration smugly humming away while all my pithy prose, and someday-I'm-going-to-try-this recipes, and salient cartoons were jammed into a dark, dark drawer.

The last time I had ever confronted an unclad icebox was on October 3, 1973. On October 4, my first child discovered crayons. For the next four years the appliance was nearly mummified by a series of tableaux in which all seemed to be titled "And this is a house, and this is the mommy, and this is the sun . . ." As those began to dwindle, other nefarious items got themselves magnetized to the door. Brownie meeting schedules, for instance. God knows there is nothing quite so ominous as knowing every time you reach in for an ice cream bar, you will see that there are only thirty-seven more days left till it's your turn to be Brownie leader. It's enough to make you diet.

The best fridge-o-bilia, of course, are *The New Yorker* cartoons. There is one that has had the place of honor in our home for ten years. It shows a couple at the marriage counselor, and the man is explaining, "We're incompatible. She's an asshole, and I'm not!" Seeing that has always made me feel better.

But I do not feel better now. Not with a naked icebox. I miss all those unused coupons that mock my pretensions at austerity. I miss my curled and jaundiced sign that sagely urges, "Feel The Fear . . . And Do It Anyway." And I have come to the conclusion that naked iceboxes are for *House Beautiful.* Real iceboxes don't go starkers. Their function isn't just to refrigerate, it's to pontificate. I want my icebox to offer up some wisdom, some support, some nagging. I want an icebox that's combination rabbi and mother.

Bring on those broccoli magnets . . .

Boys in the Girls' Bathroom

At what point do you stop letting your little boy use the ladies room and start going by himself into the mens room when you're in a public place? Even in the "olden days," when milk cartons only had pictures of cows and not of missing children, that had to be a major moment of maternal trepidation.

I know, I know. What *isn't* a major moment of maternal trepidation? I mean look at all the torment we treat ourselves to while bearing witness to all the ordinary rites of passage: our kid's first day at school, first goldfish floating on top of the tank, first exclusion from a classmate's birthday party, first bout with unrequited crushes . . . All of those provide wonderful fodder for keeping our anguish quotient nice and elevated.

So surely, even in days of yore, when our mothers pointed our little brothers toward the mens room that first time and said, "Now Benjy, I'll be waiting right outside," their hearts must have gone on hold until little Benjy toddled out in one piece.

Interestingly, all the little Benjys made that journey at a considerably younger age then than they do now. For two reasons. First of all, those were the days when little boys were being incessantly browbeaten to be "little men" and God-forbid-any-son-of-mine-would-play-with-dolls (or be seen coming out of a "powder" room.) And secondly, there's the milk-carton factor. It wasn't always a world where every child was at risk. Thus, by four or five years old, most of the little Benjys in America had gone by themselves down the long beige corridor to the mysteries behind the door marked "Men."

But today it's not mystery that lurks behind the door—it's menace. So the ladies' rooms of public places are filled with little six-, seven-, and even eight-year-old boys whose moms are more than reluctant to let them march down that long beige corridor alone. It's a real quandry. Bring them with you to the ladies room and endure a triple whammy of discomfort—yours, your son's, and all the other ladies who consider the facilities to be a respite from people (even small people) of the male persuasion. Or let them go down the corridor alone, and try not to remember that you ever saw the movie *Witness*.

Last week my friend Ellen took the second course of action. It was not optional. Matthew, her seven-year-old, absolutely put his foot down and said NO to the ladies room at Sears. So Ellen reluctantly took Matthew to the mens room door and issued those three timeworn, tremulous words, "I'm right outside."

Seven, count them, seven, interminable minutes later, little Matthew sauntered out. For the first time in his gritty little life, the kid decided to wash his hands and then wait till they were bone dry under the blower. When he finally came out, Ellen knew one thing for sure. That Matthew's bladder couldn't have been nearly as relieved as her heart.

Ellen says she's learned two things from this experience. 1) To never let Matthew indulge in any liquid refreshment either directly before or during the time spent in a stadium, an airport, or a department store. And 2) that as far as she's concerned, no boy is old enough to go off to a mens room alone, unless, maybe, he's on his honeymoon.

Beach-Blanket
Blasters

I love the beach. But every time I go there, I suffer an inordinate amount of pain. It's not the pain of sunburn, it's not even the pain of having to reveal a pair of gelatinous thighs to the world at large —it's the pain of being aurally assaulted by those colossal stereophonic radios. These elephantine boxes seem to be as integral a part of the beach attire of America's youth as the bottom of their bikinis.

Those blasted ghetto blasters have devoured every remaining segment of unused and silent airwave so there is not even a morsel of quietude left along the shores of America. I challenge you to find three square inches of sand anywhere that is not throbbing with the insistent rhythms of Duran Duran and Cyndi Lauper.

The music isn't bad. But it's the volume and scope and *inescapability* of it that can drive a beach lover off the beach. Whatever happened to Walkmans? Admittedly, wearing a headset to the beach may cause the ears to sweat, may ruin a tan line, and may make socializing a bit more difficult, but there would be a multitude of benefits. Benefit number one would be not having old ladies like me come over and ask that the music be turned down. Benefit number two would be not having old ladies like me come over again and say, Listen, kid, I really mean it. And benefit number three would be not having to confront the lifeguard who I would send over as my ultimate weapon for enforcing the original request.

Surely the kids wouldn't schlepp around ten pounds of sound

equipment were some serious sociological goals not being achieved —goals such as (1) boxes are a surefire conversation starter. Just as a dog on a leash used to provide a guaranteed opener for a bit of repartee, these portable shrines to technology offer up myriad opportunities for getting a bit of snappy patter rolling, i.e., "Is that a four-track or an eight?" or "Did you get that at Radio Shack?" (2) Boxes provide a continuing opportunity to sing along and prove you know the words of every song in the top 40, a prerequisite if you plan to maintain even a modicum of self-esteem between the ages of thirteen and eighteen. (3) Boxes are useful because they limit the long-term amount of conversational savvy you are expected to have. If you get a great FM station, it's possible not to have to talk for twenty or thirty minutes at a time, other than turning to your companions and saying, "I love this song" or "I'm so sick of this song." Boxes are a great boon for shy people. (4) Boxes help keep most adults at bay. This is self-explanatory.

I am sure that the brigades of blasters are not on the beach with the intent of screwing up my afternoon any more than smokers smoke with the intent of fouling my air. But in the same way that passive smoking is harmful to a person's biological equilibrium, passive rock and rolling is harmful to a person's mental equilibrium. For many of us, beaches are where we go to escape, so it is very distressing to find the very thing we sought to escape—the cacophony of contemporary life—saturating our ostensible sanctuary. We can tolerate little children squealing and whining and kicking up sand—that goes with the territory. But being subjected to the decibels of these gargantuan sound systems truly taxes the tolerance of any grown-up worth his Valium prescription.

I've been complaining about this to my friend Claudine for weeks. And she called me the other day to give me great news. She's found a beach where blasters are prohibited. There's only one drawback . . . bathing suits are prohibited, too. It really helped me put things in perspective.

Because I'd rather listen to ZZ Top than go without mine any day.

Lift Illogic

Everybody does it. Or knows someone who's done it. Or thinks they know someone who's done it. But no one seems to want to fess up.

It remains the ultimate indelicate question.

It is almost 1990 and you still can't say to someone, "You know you look really great. And I hope you don't mind my asking, but I've been thinking of having my eyes done, and wondered if by any chance you've ever been to a plastic surgeon."

You can't do that, because even though it is fundamentally a compliment, and even though you are telling someone that she looks terrific, you are saying to her that she couldn't possibly look that terrific naturally, so she must have bought terrific.

And somehow, bought terrific isn't as nearly as terrific as natural terrific. Which is pretty silly when you consider that hardly anybody remains naturally terrific. Because acknowledging that you had plastic surgery, still, at some subliminal level says you're vain, neurotic, and self-indulgent. It's okay to admit you're working out in order to keep nature in check, and it's okay to admit you're dieting to keep nature in check, but it's still not quite okay to say you went snip snip/tuck tuck to keep nature in check.

Oh it's okay to say it if you're Joan Rivers or Phyllis Diller. It provides great material. But if you're just forty-five-year-old Mary Smith who doesn't necessarily want to look like a thirty-five-year-old Mary Smith, but more like a forty-year-old Mary Smith who just got a great night's sleep, you tend not to own up.

Even if you're fifty-six-year-old Elizabeth Taylor who has gone public about a drinking problem, you don't go public about a lift. It's one thing to own up to bad habit, it's another to own up to bad genes. Because when you go to a plastic surgeon, you aren't just paying for the improvement, you are paying for the illusion that you needed no improving in the first place. So if somebody asks you if you had something done, then you only got half of your money's worth.

That's why, even though inquiring minds want to know, everyone walks around on eggshells. And that might be the reason that half the people selecting plastic surgeons do so based on—are you ready for this—ads in the Yellow Pages! Do you believe that? It's one thing to let your fingers do the walking for a pizza, or to let your fingers do the walking for a plumber, but when you let your fingers do the walking for your face . . . now *that* is real scary.

Almost as scary as each time you've said to someone, "I'm thinking of doing my eyes," not one person has said, "You? Are you kidding? You don't need to do your eyes!" Not one person.

So there you sit . . . still left wondering how to ask The Question. And that's only the half of it. Once you have finally uttered the most awkward question you've ever had to ask, then you're going to have to ask the doc the second most awkward . . .

As long as he's doing the wrinkles, could he please do the zits, too?

Life Beyond the Slopes

There is one social shortcoming I harbor that has been a source of inordinate ignominy over the years. I don't ski. In the olden days, when our mommies wore seamed stockings and our daddies watched Milton Berle, this was not considered a serious handicap. Especially if you lived in the Midwest where there are no geological proturbances much higher than a curb. It was perfectly okay to grow up in Chicago and not even think about putting on boots that were double your body weight, attaching two long planks on the bottom, keeping your knees bent for hours on end, trying to remain vertical against great geophysical forces battling freezing temperatures and madding crowds, and calling the experience great fun.

But somewhere along the line this changed. Even if you were living in Podunk Plains, Kansas, it became mandatory to learn to ski. Vail stories, broken limb stories, ski instructor named Gunter stories became regulation offerings in everybody's repertoire. You could get away with saying that you didn't like the Beatles; you could get away with saying that you didn't like *Portnoy's Complaint*, but about twenty years ago, it became impossible to get away with saying you didn't like skiing. People would recoil from you as if you had just announced you were starting a fan club for Hermann Goering.

So I tried to keep it under wraps. I mean I really did try to like skiing. But the conditions were never really quite right. First of all, my debut on the slopes took place in a less than idyllic setting. The Bronx. Somehow schussing down the urban alps of Van Cortlandt Park just a few short steps from the fierce tremors of the IRT subway left something to be desired in terms of ambience.

Also, I personally found it difficult to be enchanted with a sport in which great volumes of money must be paid before you are even permitted to fall down and look stupid. It is no small deal to fork out for skis 'n' poles 'n' boots, 'n' snowpants, 'n' lessons, 'n' lift tickets. No sirree, humiliation does not come cheaply.

Which brings up the third thing I hated about skiing. The myth that anyone can do it. That it's easy. Look at all those little kids whooshing by in that popular full-tilt, knees-locked, feet-parallel position that goes counter to every posture class and physiological configuration you've ever encountered. Skiing is not only hard, it's anatomically perverse. In addition to being expensive and hardly ever convenient. No, my final verdict on skiing was an unqualified *ix-nay*.

So you can imagine the terror that crept into my life when my boy kidlet started nagging me a few years ago about skiing. "Mommy, can't I just try it once?" For seven years I held him off. This year, a series of heinous circumstances colluded to make it impossible to continue the stalemate.

So we schlepped up to Wisconsin, to some ersatz little slopes with ersatz snow, and genuine instructors. At noon the teacher returned and said the kid was doing so great that he had just headed for the slopes. I was aghast. By two o'clock when he wasn't back I began to sweat. Clearly he'd found his calling, and I was about to spend the next several years drinking coffee in the ski lodges of America. By three o'clock, when he hadn't come back, I was really depressed—the financial implications alone of supporting his new sportive habit were paralyzing.

Finally, at three-thirty, the purple-cheeked, runny-nosed junior Jean-Claude came walking down the mountain carrying his skis, covered in snow, and minus one glove and one pole. He walked directly into the lodge, threw the whole mess down on the floor, and said with the kind of petulance and rage that only a mother could love, "I tried it, Mom. I really did. But I hated it."

There is a God.

Post Plug-In Blues

Okay. Everything has been opened and I'll wager you anything that somewhere in the loot is some wonderful new device that has to be plugged in. And I'm just warning you to think twice before you do it. Because whether it's a new VCR, or a new espresso machine, or a new computer, once you plug it in, you will regret it.

Oh you won't regret it right away. At first you will just be afraid of it. Till you figure out how it works. But once you do that, the trouble begins. Because it will become a part of your life. And once it becomes a part of your life, you begin to rely on it a lot. And once you realize how reliant you are on it, you will realize how truly you love it. And then, and only then, when it knows you love it and *you can't live without it,* will it one day very quietly, and very effectively, just nail you.

It will simply glitch out. One little thing will go wrong with it. And you will die. You will go insane. You will feel the bottom of your world dropped out. For instance, let's talk about the answering machine I got for Christmas three years ago. It was, as all first answering machines are, something of a philosophical capitulation. We all know these machines are fundamentally a bit reprehensible, and yet ultimately we sell out. It is not a moment we are proud of.

Neither is the moment that occurs thirteen to sixteen months later—when the little bugger breaks down and we start frothing at the mouth because for the next two weeks while it is at the answering-machine hospital, we will actually have to exist without it. The fact that we existed without it for four decades has absolutely no bearing on the degree of equanimity with which we deal with this two-week sabbatical. We actually feel quite convinced that a life without an answering machine is not a life worth living.

Or take the VCR. Actually don't. Because if you take it away, for a day or for a week or for, GOD FORBID, ten days, your entire family could collapse from despair. Once a VCR enters your life, it becomes as vital to your well-being as the presence of clean air and a great sushi bar. You hate yourself for being so dependent. You hate yourself for feeling so bereft. But, most of all, you hate IT, for pointing out in such a cruel and explicit fashion that in the ongoing power struggle between man and technology, the former is not in first place. It becomes quite clear just who is pushing whose buttons.

Trust me. I know of what I speak. Ten days ago I thought my entire world was hunky-dory. The next day I was suicidal. It didn't take much. The letter *e* on my computer didn't compute. Have you ever tried to write without the letter *e?* Have you ever tried to exist without the letter *e?* See? You can't even write "exist" without it. It doesn't seem like much, but the hard, fast metaphysical truth is that without the letter *e,* I was a zero on the ticktacktoe board of life. I could no more write on a yellow pad again than go back to believing in the tooth fairy. I was rendered totally nonfunctional by one twenty-sixth of the alphabet.

So remember—modern conveniences only look like they offer freedom. In truth they offer just the opposite. Think about that before you become a high-tech slave. Caveat plugger-inner.

The Plot Doesn't Thicken

I'm all in favor of being organized. But some people go too far. Some people cook Thanksgiving dinner weeks in advance and then just defrost it and zap it on the big day. Yech.

People who cook turkeys in advance have trouble dealing with the future. So they try to put the future into the present, and figure by doing that they are on top of the situation. Of course how can you be on top of a situation if you think it's actually okay to serve frozen, rezapped turkey?

Now I am not a person who has trouble dealing with the future. I have no trouble with it, because I don't deal with it. I ignore it. Just like most people. I feel qualified to say that because, in a recent unscientific survey I have just run, everyone said "no" to the following question. The question was, "Have you purchased your final resting place?"

The reason I asked this question was I had just discovered something appalling about some people I know. These people have not only gone to the cemetery and made an advance purchase on the little plot of ground where they'd like to rest their bones for all eternity . . . *they have actually purchased their stones.* And engraved on these stones are their names, dates of birth, and, on the last line . . . well, all that remains is to fill in the blank.

I find this kind of jangling. I figure people like that are either hyperorganized or they must have gotten a really great buy on granite that week. In either case, I wouldn't want to eat the turkey they're serving on Thanksgiving Day. But this did get me to think-ing. Why, when we do not consider it creepy to buy life insurance, do we refuse to take the concept one step further and buy ourselves a plot?

Cemetery guys will tell you there are many sound reasons to purchase a plot while we are in a "pre-need" mode. Reasons like:

We can make a decision calmly rather than during a time when we are in a highly emotional state. Well that may be true on paper, but come on . . . no matter when you discuss it, the topic of eternal resting places is going to churn up some major emotions. Calm not being one of them.

Families decide on what furniture, car, and home to buy to-gether; we should do the same with burial plots. Well, "decide on" is one way to put it. "Hassle over" is another. You just know that burial grounds would be yet one more arena for domestic dissen-sion. And the last thing most of us need is a knock-down/drag-out on whether we want to spend eternity at the fountain end of the premises or whether to opt for a tomb with a view.

We won't make any mistakes. We'll be carrying out the de-ceased's exact wishes. Perhaps. But think of the flip side. This is a wonderful opportunity to finally get the last word.

Of course the cemetery guys will give you a million more reasons. Property always goes up, better selection, avoid emotional overspending, etc. etc., etc. Which is all well and good, except it all falls on deaf ears anyway. No way is the average person going to start shopping plots. And why should we?

Most of us just don't make a habit of buying something that we're never really going to need.

Short and Not So Sweet

It has not been easy to be a short person these past few weeks. Because some guy at Stanford ran a study and found that tall kids are smarter than short kids. Not an especially thrilling thing to hear when you are a five-foot-one columnist making her living based on ostensibly keen mental observations.

The thing is, lots of us short people actually like being short. Of course tall people never believe us when we tell them this. Behind our short, stubby little backs they whisper, "That poor thing has a serious case of denial." And this truly rotten finding no doubt compounds their skepticism.

Granted, there are some things about short that are not swell. One is that no matter how sophisticated you may dress or how sophisticated you may be, people will always describe you as "cute." "Cute" is okay when you are twelve. Or even when you are twenty. But like cheap wine, "cute" does not age well. "Pretty" grows into "lovely," and "lovely" grows into "attractive." Even "ugly" grows into "interesting" and "interesting" grows into "handsome." But "cute" doesn't grow into anything. It just hangs around getting more embarrassing by the decade. Ask Billy Crystal, or Debbie Reynolds, or . . . me.

That's another thing about being short. The names. Look above. Bill*y*, and Debb*ie*, and Jud*y*. No way did we ever have a chance to be William or Deborah or Judith. I used to say that names were destiny, and that if my parents had named me Samantha, I would have been tall and Gentile. Now I know better. Now I know I'd just have been a short, Jewish girl named Sammy.

No big deal. We short people can put up with a lot. Because there are still three very important reasons we love being short. First of all, it's so cheap. Short people can shop in the preteen department. Years ago this wouldn't have been possible since grown-up women wore bona fide Mommy outfits and grown-up men wore bona fide Daddy outfits. Then came jeans and tennis shoes—the staples of the American wardrobe. You can save hundreds of dollars a year if you are willing to try on jeans in dressing rooms that are wallpapered with posters of Madonna and Rob Lowe.

Secondly, there is the issue of hope. Everybody knows that there are moments in life when the grass always does seem greener. Thus, occasionally, short people may fantasize about being taller or tall people may fantasize about being shorter. In these instances short people have a distinct advantage over tall people. Short people can always hope against hope for a possible growth spurt. Tall people can hardly ever hope for the inverse.

Lastly, short people tend to be overachievers. This means if you are short, you frequently behave in an obnoxious, overbearing fashion. Tall people think that you are behaving like this because you are feeling short and inadequate. Thus, they will forgive you for your inexcusable behavior. They figure you are simply overcompensating. Of course you know that is not the case. You know perfectly well that you love being short.

And the only reason that you are behaving that way is that quite simply, you actually ARE obnoxious and overbearing.

The Hardest Ones to Write

I don't believe in condolence cards. They're too staunch a way to respond to a trembly situation.

I figure, even if someone has only grazed though your life superficially, if you're jangled enough by their loss to want to send them a condolence card, then you're capable of sitting down and writing a real note.

They don't write easy. Because there are No Words. There are just good intentions, impotence, and sadness. And sometimes rage. You don't see condolence cards with rage. But the note I have to write today, the one I've been putting off for several days, is going to be one speckled with rage.

Someone murdered my friend. He lived in Washington, D.C. I hadn't seen him in thirteen years. Somewhere along the line we even stopped sending Christmas cards. But he was still my friend. And someone murdered him.

That doesn't make me unique. Not if you consider the wretched statistics. Nearly 22,000 Americans are murdered each year. That means there are a lot of people who have to write *this* kind of condolence note. You begin to feel that you've written at least one of every sort of condolence note there is by the time you hit forty or fifty. By that time, someone you know has lost a parent; someone you know has lost a sibling; someone you know has lost a spouse; someone you know has lost a child; and now this, someone you know has lost someone to violent crime.

I don't know. I figured four weeks ago when I sat down to say something "right" to a woman whose twelve-year-old had just died of cancer that that one would be the hardest one I ever had to write. I almost succumbed that time and bought a card. But there was nothing to choose from all those selections of prepackaged compassion that wasn't leaning pretentiously toward austere or precariously toward maudlin. But I was so paralyzed about writing this woman. I hadn't seen her in years, and I didn't really even know her daughter, so what could I possibly say?

Only what I felt. It took an hour. One hour for maybe four or five lines that someone at Norcross might want to set in iambic pentameter. One hour just to say all the things that always come out sounding so inadequate. Even when you're a writer.

And this one is even harder to write. My friend in Washington was no ordinary man. After graduating magna cum laude and Phi Beta Kappa from the University of Florida, he came to Washington, D.C., and founded two Montessori schools. He and his wife, after adopting one child, had another, and were Sunday school teachers at their church. He recently went back to graduate school to get his doctorate in clinical psychology. Last year he was given an internship in the state hospital at Annapolis, where the director said, "He was one of the best interns I've ever had in twenty years." To help with the bills, my friend moonlighted as a cabdriver. Every fifteenth ride he'd give for free. He'd tell his passenger to keep the money and give it to charity. Two weeks ago, one passenger shot him and then set fire to his cab.

For this one there are no cards. This is one of the ones where you have to sit down and write from your inners. I never knew what a difference that made until I was on the receiving end of the condolences when my father died. Every morning my mother and I would dive into that mail. We'd read briskly through the polite store-bought sympathy cards. And then we'd settle in to relish the "real ones"—the handwritten, hard-thought, wrenched-from-within ones that made us laugh and cry all at once.

The note I write isn't going to assuage the grief of my friend's family. It would be presumptuous to think that any kind of prose could do that. But the note I write will *matter*. Spending that hour always matters a lot more than spending seventy-five cents. What you have to do is a lot harder than buying a Hallmark if you care enough to do the very best.

Sprinting Toward Geezer-dom

When Paul Newman turned sixty a few years back, just about everyone expressed major amounts of incredulity. No one could quite believe he was THAT OLD. It doesn't really come packaged as a number. It comes packaged in a moment.

As in "Hey, Mom. How did people go shopping in the olden days when they didn't have malls?" One searing sentence like that is all it takes to let you know that as far as some people are concerned, you were born about an hour and a half after triceratops.

Most of us make our way fairly deep into the chronology of our twenties, thirties, or forties and still see ourselves fairly firmly ensconced in a youth mode. We think that even though we're walking around with a briefcase, a mortgage, and a divorce decree or two, we're really just playing dress-up as a genuine adult. I know plenty of people with salt-and-pepper hair who still refer to their parent's friends as "the grown-ups." Until they have their moment. Which thrusts them involuntarily and instantaneously splat in the middle of geezer-dom.

It happened to my thirty-eight year-old friend Tim a couple of weeks ago at the hockey game. Tim is clearly several decades away from retirement. And he always figured that going to the hockey game with the guys was just further evidence that he must be not-quite-an-adult. (Actually, anyone who has ever been to a professional hockey game and observed the fans, would find it difficult to disagree with this premise.) One of the regulars in Tim's block of seats was sick, so a nineteen-year-old spotted the empty seat and asked if he could park himself there. No problem. Until halftime when Tim headed for the concession stand and on the way back passed the nineteen-year-old, whose pals were saying to him, "Where ya been? Come sit with us . . ."

"Naw," he said, poking one of the guys in the ribs as if he was telling them the greatest joke ever. "I'm sittin' down there with this bunch of *old* guys." They're still finding shards of Tim's shattered ego when they sweep the floors of the arena. The man hasn't been the same since.

No one is, once you have your moment. That fleeting encounter with the nasty, naked reality that you have irrefutably said *ciao* to your salad days. That nasty little revelation which lets you know once and for all that you ain't being considered for the ingenue or Romeo part anymore.

It happens to everyone. And we all remember the precise moment. Here's what some people said when I asked them to complete the following sentence: "I knew I was old —————"

"the first time someone called me 'sir.' "

"when I saw the cellulite and just didn't care anymore."

"when Louis Jourdan started to play the Maurice Chevalier part in *Gigi*."

"when I turned on the Grammys and didn't know anyone except John Denver and Tina Turner."

"when I wasn't even pregnant, and some kid offered me a seat on the bus."

"when I realized my medicine chest had more stuff in it than is on my cosmetic shelf."

"when I saw that a '57 Chevy, my car in high school, is considered a classic. I mean if my car is a classic, what the hell does that make me?"

"when the station I have on my car radio is the same as the one they're playing in my dentist's waiting room."

The Threat-and-Forget School of Discipline

President Reagan recently went on record with a rather brazen parental lament: "I wish spanking were more fashionable these days." Of course comments like these cause thunderous gasps among those of us who have fancied ourselves the ultimate enlightened child raisers.

Spanking just isn't something the 1980s parent considers as a standard option. Instead we go in for the Threat-and-Forget School of Discipline. The Threat-and-Forget School of Discipline offers two wondrous advantages. The threat part guarantees that our children will be menaced with a fabulous variety of punitive measures, not just a boringly regressive corporal one like spanking. And the forget part guarantees that the parent need not follow through because he can never recall what odious deprivation he promised the child. Those of us who have become seasoned veterans of the Threat-and-Forget School of Discipline need not ever worry about losing our niche in the Wimpy Parents Hall of Fame. I personally have a guaranteed lifetime chair there.

It is very difficult to remember what dire consequences I have pledged to administer to the little nippers because the proposed punitive measures are almost always issued (1) in a fit of pique or (2) when I'm on the phone. Admonitions issued in either of these circumstances are always highly inventive, but, alas, they are always inappropriate. For instance, when it's 10 P.M. and a six-year-old child emerges from the bedroom for a glass of water for the seventeenth time while you are having a heart-wrenching conversation with your best friend about her divorce, it's not uncommon to find yourself yelling, "If you don't get back in that bed right this minute," (pause) . . . "I am not sending you to college."

Ultimatums like this accomplish very little, other than proving your creativity and long-range-planning capabilities. In addition to the punishment somewhat exceeding the crime, there's an irrelevance factor that makes this kind of maxi-threat nigh onto ludicrous. Also ludicrous, however, is the mini-threat. The mini-threat arises from a chronically annoying situation, such as the sight of a teenager's squalor-strewn room. You locate the child in front of the TV and the mini-threat issued usually sounds like this: "If you don't get that room cleaned up right now, there will be no TV for" (pause) . . . (Do you want to deal in days or weeks or what? This is always so confusing) . . . "36 hours." As soon as the edict is announced, it's wise to develop instant amnesia because these no-TV ultimatums frequently overlap no-going-out ultimatums. The very thought of a teenager home for days on end with no amusements permitted him but listening to his rock music defies the imagination.

Of course the queen mother of chastisements issued by those of us in the Threat-and-Forget School is the "If you don't blah blah blah (fill in the blank) there will be no (a) birthday party, (b) Christmas presents, (c) Halloween. Listen, any kid worth his weight in magic markers on the walls or scissored-off living room curtains knows this is the ultimate in empty threats. If he's an hour over four years old he knows that the one who undergoes the most agony and torture if he's denied holiday privileges isn't going to be him. Surely it would be simpler to spank a child than watch him writhe through a party-less birthday.

However, we Threat-and-Forgetters aren't about to take the easy route. We're determined to be modern, sophisticated, and wise. Everyone knows the experts say consistency is the key to successful parenting. That's why us Threat-and-Forgetters are such terrific parents. Our children can count on us to be consistently inconsistent. No wonder they are so well disciplined and secure.

Beyond Handcuffs

Personally I've always felt that handcuffs would be a great topic to write on. I mean you can just write about kids and guys and money and thighs for just so long, you know? Handcuffs, on the other hand, have a certain *je ne sais quoi*—a little menacing, a little sexy, a little bizarre.

So the idea was real simple—just cram a pair of handcuffs into the old purse, and every time I rifled through it for my wallet, let the handcuffs tumble out and then take a reading on the folk bearing witness to this special moment in aberrant behavior. I'm not saying that this little experiment would have merited a Nobel prize in science, but surely the results would have provided for some whimsical prose.

However, when I bounced the idea off several of my colleagues, folks whom I had always assumed approached life with an overdose of irreverence and sass, a communal gasp was heard. Handcuffs indeed! Girl, you do that and everyone is going to just assume that you were hoping for the Kim Basinger part in *9 1/2 Weeks*. Your readers will not be able to deal with that, they said. Your readers want you just where you've always been—still driving car pools, but doing it in a miniskirt. Suburban schizoid, if you will.

So I acquiesced. I abandoned handcuffs. And instead I turned for my experiment to something a tad more "now"—the condom card. The condom card is a gold plastic card that looks almost like a revered gold credit card—only instead of being imprinted with your name, it is imprinted with the truly discreet inquiry: "May I please have a box of Trojan Brand Condoms."

I kid you not. One small sliver of plastic that makes it possible to circumvent an entire rite of passage. Mark Klein, vice-president of the Family Products division of Carter-Wallace, the manufacturer of Trojans, says the point of the card is to take an inherently embarrassing moment and make it a bit less angsty. Can't you just see showing it to your friendly local pharmacist, then watch him stifle his laughter, head for the back room, and finally bellow, "Hey, lady, you want the lambskin or the ribbed ones?" Or can't you just see some snooty waiters nearly die of apoplexy when you mistakenly pull the card out and try to pay for dinner with it?

So I couldn't wait to try it out in my neighborhood. Granted it took me a couple of weeks to work up the nerve. But yesterday I was in one of our local emporiums and when I went to pay for my purchases I let the gold card slip to the counter. I figured by the time I got to the front door, the cashier would have read it and the whole place would have gone up for grabs. I figured my reputation would be sullied and there would be enough material for a "Candid Camera" special. I figured wrong.

All that happened was that the kid came running out of the store and said, "Mrs. Markey, Mrs. Markey, you forgot your condom card."

God, I love the eighties.

The Friendship That Fits

I just finished reading my seventh women's magazine in the past thirty-six hours. This can be rough on a girl's emotional equilibrium. Mainly because women's magazines these days are filled with three main things: articles on how to live with a man, articles on how to live without a man, and articles on condoms (in case you haven't decided which of the first two categories you're definitely in yet). Then come the usual articles on how to have a truly wonderful career, how to have truly wonderful children, and how to have truly wonderful thighs. Grim I tell you, incredibly grim.

But the grimmest of all (next to the recipe for snail lasagna) was an article in this month's *Working Woman* on how to "fit in" friends. You heard me right. I said "fit in." Not "be with." Not "hang out with." Not "enjoy." But "fit in." As in "Oh God, my work is so significant and my life is so crammed with important obligations that I couldn't possibly stop and say the heck with it for just two or three hours and sit around with old Mabel over a long lunch or dinner just catching up . . . So how can I *fit her in?* I've got it. I *do* have to take my car in for a 50,000-mile tune-up, so maybe when I take it into the garage, she'd like to come on along and that way I can *fit her in.*"

Because that's what this article actually suggests. In fact actual shrinks actually suggest that a really swell solution to "fitting in" friends is to ask your friend to join you while you knock a few disgusting chores off your list. Dusting, for instance. In fact hard as this is to fathom, the actual shrink, who actually suggests this, actually DOES this. She calls up one of her girlfriends and says, "Hey Charlene, I've got a bunch of housekeeping to do and since I haven't seen you in ages, hows about you come on over and we can kibbutz and clean at the same time?"

What a great idea. How could anyone refuse? Imagine having a friend think so much of you that even though she could do her vacuuming alone, she's actually inviting you over to help her out. Of course, God forbid that she skips the vacuuming for a night and the two of you just sit around and get silly over girl talk and margaritas. Not allowed for today's working women. Busy, busy, busy. No time to probe the potholes of each other's minds, no time to savor the anecdotes of each other's daily lives, no time to give full attention to another person you ostensibly value when you can give them a demi-dose of attention instead and get your bathroom swabbed too. Forget the tea, now it's *Ty-D-Bol and Sympathy*.

Oh ladies, ladies, ladies. What has happened to our priorities? How did we get so confused? Friends and freneticism do not go hand in hand. Friendships are built on compassion—not compression; on time spent—not time used; on savoring things together—not scouring things together.

I tell you, if a friend of mine ever invites me over and hands me a can of Drano, it will be a whole lot more than sludge that's headed down the drain.

Cruisin' with My Honey

I bet I hadn't seen a sight like that in ten, fifteen years. And was it ever a sight for sore eyes.

Cruising along in a huge battered bruiser of a car right in front of me was a real Dating Couple. The guy was at the wheel and PLASTERED right next to him, shoulder to shoulder, thigh to thigh, was his little honey. It was wonderful, it was retro, it was the Full American Bandstand Look.

Wooooosh! came the memories. Memories of the biggest dating decision of all if you were once a *vrai* fifties girl. Not what do I wear, and not what do I talk about, but the big one . . . WHERE DO I SIT? It was without question the major philosophical statement of a female dater's life.

Because it said so much. Every inch closer to the guy or closer to the door bespoke bushels about how the evening was going, and even more importantly . . . how the evening would end. It was the ultimate MPG—Makeout Potential Gage.

Here's how it worked. The guy picked you up, and as you'd head for the car, he'd say with typical teen-person decisiveness, "So-whaddya-wanna-do?" You of course would respond with commensurate teen-person decisiveness and say, "I dunno." Then he'd open the door of the vehicle. And—depending on where you sat— the entire course of the evening was destiny.

If you sat decorously in the middle, he'd know he was in for at least one movie theater and two hamburgers before anything hormonal was on the horizon. If you sat a tad to the left of that, he'd know he could probably skip the burgers and do just fine in the horizontal department anyway. If you actually sat even to the left of that, welding your throbbing adolescent loin to his, he'd know he could pass on both the burgers and movie theater and head directly for the drive-in. However, if you were a DDH (dandy door hugger), this guy knew he was in for an extremely long evening.

And then in 1963 all that ended. Bucket seats were introduced. And suddenly girls were mandatorily removed a decorous eighteen inches from their gentleman callers. No longer was a female able to send out any clear signals to these poor, pubescent seducers-in-training. No longer was there any barometer for a guy to read. It was a truly chilling moment in the History of Dating.

And of course it got worse. Because then there were seat belts, and while they are extremely terrific for driving safety, they do make it a bit hard for all those befuddled 1988 guys trying to take a romance reading on their 1988 girls.

I guess that's why seeing those two in the car ahead of me, with about as much space between them as two halves of a Popsicle made my little Annette Funicello heart leap, and made me feel real nostalgic.

So I pulled up next to the old beater where these two were bonding in the front seat and noticed much to my surprise that there was nothing nostalgic about them at all. This was a real '80s couple.

It was two girls.

It's Only a Dream, Dear

Last night I had about the best dream a girl could have.

I dreamed that Jane Fonda finally gave it up.

Yup, I dreamed that after nearly a decade of setting the curve on fitness fanaticism, our Ms. Fonda simply threw in the old video towel. That at long last this woman, this icon of low-impact intensity, said, "Hey, guys, I quit. I've had it with being disciplined, dedicated, and terminally divine." I dreamed that one morning Jane Fonda woke up, and said so long forever to her size six leather jeans, and headed out the door for a six-pack from Dunkin' Donuts.

And who can blame the woman? Jane Fonda has probably been hungry for years. A friend of mine was once in a green room waiting to go on a talk show with her. It happened to be lunchtime so a deli spread was put out for the guests. And do you know what Jane Fonda had for lunch? Jane Fonda had half a banana. Not a whole banana. Not even three quarters of a banana. But one half of one measly banana. And when someone commented on the, uh, microscopic aspect of this meal, Jane simply shrugged her outstandingly svelte shoulders and said, "I always have half a banana for lunch."

What kind of life, I ask you, is a half-a-banana life? I mean there has to be a point where you look back over years of half-a-banana lunches and figure out, hey, even monkeys have a better deal. Where you say to yourself, So what if I look great in a leotard? So what if at this very minute I have seven—count them seven—

videos on the market? And so what if in addition to looking great in a leotard, and having seven videos on the market, I happen to be extremely rich? Because you know what? I'm hungry. And I am extremely tired. And, I am going to chuck it. I am going to trade it all in for an order of cheese fries.

Yes, at long last Jane Fonda was letting go. Jane Fonda was giving in. Jane Fonda was shutting up. At long last Jane Fonda was releasing the women of America from the tyranny of the taut.

It was truly fab. I dreamed Jane Fonda finally put out the video we've all been waiting for: "Jane Fonda Learns to Live with Cellulite." There she was lolling about in an old robe on her Barcalounger—channel changer in one hand and a bag of barbecue potato chips in the other.

I know, I know it was only a dream. But don't tell me it could never come true. That's what they said to the Wright Brothers, and to Alexander Graham Bell, and to all those other people whose dreams came true.

Anyway, you've got to admit, it was the world's greatest dream. Because I dreamed that Jane Fonda was no longer going for the burn. She was going for the burnout.

And the women of America rejoiced.

Oh, Grow Up!

I hate to admit this, but there is definitely one thing our parents did a whole lot better than we do. They grown-upped better. They owned up being grown-ups right away. Unlike us folks who are currently somewhere between thirty and fifty who just can't absorb the fact that we are indeed genuine adults.

Because even though we have acquired all the trappings of grown-updom—i.e., condos, jobs, families, lawyers, lawnmowers, and insurance policies—we're just aghast that anyone might even consider us to be a grown-up. The very fact that we use the word *grown-up*, indicates that we have more than a mild case of arrested development.

It's almost as if we think it's kind of cute to resist grown-updom. Actually, it's kind of uncute. It's kind of *very* uncute. Not to mention it's quite pathetic. I think if I read one more column or article by someone who has just turned forty and can't believe that he or she is a certifiable adult, I may have to reach for my airsick bag.

I mean why is it so difficult for adults my age to feel like adults? Look at our parents. They embraced adulthood about an hour after their twenty-first birthday. Grown-ups in the fifties and sixties loved being grown-ups. Those guys couldn't wait to go out and put on their Daddy Hats and get all responsibili-tied up. They took one look at adulthood, at the freedom it offered and the ac-countability it required, and they said, Yessir, that's for me. They pretty much decided if they were going to wear grown-up clothes then, yup, that must mean they were grown-ups.

But we just pretend we're dressing up. We're just having an awful time acknowledging that terrible and most eternal of truths: that this, my friends, is indeed Our Time. And that no matter how many trillions of dollars we've spent at the shrink—we *are* our parents. Why do we keep fighting this?

I suppose some of it can be explained because we came of age at a time when adults were viewed with more than a pinch of suspicion. It's hard to want to be a grown-up, when you grew up under the impression that people over thirty couldn't be trusted. And it's real hard to want to be a grown-up when you grew up under the impression that grown-up means *old.* Which is only somewhat worse than what grown-up really means, which is *mature.* No matter—both of those are four-letter words to our generation.

Of course none of this bodes well for the next generation. How would you like to have been raised by a mom and dad who refused to be the grown-ups? Who insisted with almost moronic monotony that behind those veined and jiggly thighs and/or that bald pate and gelatinous paunch there was still a zany high school sophomore clawing to get out? It really is a remarkably unattractive mindset.

So what do you say, ladies and gentlemen . . . can we do it? Can we give up our misplaced assumptions that we're still in the wings waiting to be called? Can we acknowledge that for better or worse this is indeed center stage? And can we face the fact that there is no such thing as a forty-year-old ingenue?

No one said you had to give up rock and roll, too.

Reunion Redux

I worked real hard on establishing some extremely low expectations. People do that when they don't want to be disappointed. And I definitely didn't want to be disappointed by my twenty-fifth high school reunion. Because the twentieth was so magical. So magical that I took it upon myself to write a book about it, give speeches about it, talk on TV about it, and in general to probably bore millions while waxing rhapsodic about the wonderfulness of it.

But I wanted people to know that twentieth reunions offer an extraordinary reprieve from insecurity. That by the time we hit thirty-eight, we are grounded enough to risk being genuinely nice to each other, genuinely interested in each other, and genuinely happy for each other. I haven't talked to a single person who went to a twentieth reunion who found it to be anything less than luminescent.

Which is why attending the twenty-fifth certainly gave me pause. It seemed a little naive, and a little greedy, and a little risky to try to get a second helping of epiphany. That's where the low expectations came in. I figured that as long as I didn't expect magic again, I would be okay. So all I expected from my twenty-fifth reunion, was "nice." And it was. It was nice.

But it was something else, too. It was incredibly *middle aged*. And that was a killer surprise . . .

I don't know what exactly it is that happens to us between thirty-eight and forty-three, but somewhere in that time zone, we definitely begin to lose it. Even in California where I went to high school, and where people go to great (translate that into "even surgical") extremes not to lose it, something gives way. I'm telling you . . . the big difference between twentieth and twenty-fifth reunions is simple. At the twentieth we are grown-ups. At the twenty-fifth we are old.

It isn't just a question of being jowlier, puffier, and paunchier. It's also a question of where we are in life. For instance, at the twentieth reunion, they gave an award to the person having the oldest child. At the twentieth reunion they gave an award to the person having the youngest child. (Which, wouldn't you just know, was split between three men with *very new, very young, very pregnant* wives.) Thus at the twentieth they're giving awards to early starters, at the twenty-fifth they're giving awards for staying power.

At the twentieth it was not surprising to see the occasional person slip outside to indulge in a bit of recreational substance abuse. At the twenty-fifth we were ordering decaffeinated coffee.

At the twentieth we were telling each other where *we* had gone to college. At the twenty-fifth we were telling each other where *our kids* were going to college. At the twentieth it was hot so we all wore shorts to the class picnic. At the twenty-fifth it was even hotter and we all wore jeans.

At the twentieth we were hoping maybe the prom queen didn't hold up. At the twenty-fifth we gleaned hope from the fact that she did. You think you need prom queens when you'e eighteen; but, honey, you don't know how much you need them until you're forty-three.

The Saturday Night
Non-Special

Tell me if I'm wrong. But it seems that one of the lovely things about getting to be "older" is the diminishment of the Saturday Night Imperative. The Saturday Night Imperative is a bit like the New Year's Eve Imperative, only instead of haunting you annually, it nails you every seven days. The Saturday Night Imperative is a weekly mandate to be engaged in some sort of festive social intercourse with one or more persons between seven and midnight on the last day of the week.

Remember all the years it had such import? From ages seventeen to twenty-five No Saturday Night Date was a cause of major consternation and shame. One could have hardly felt more stigmatized being caught shoplifting than being caught dateless in the dorm on Saturday night. There is no one who doesn't remember accepting an invitation from a total cretin and saying with a shrug of the shoulders, "Oh well, at least it's a Saturday night date." Not having a reason to wash your hair, a companion, and a destination on the eve before the sabbath has always seemed infinitely more humiliating than not having any of the above on a Sunday through Friday.

What was so special about Saturday that it had so much more clout in the loneliness-making department than any other evening of the week? Was it a holdover from the old paycheck-in-the-pocket/no-work-tomorrow ethic or did it curdle into something a bit more insidious? I think it did. I think for most of us Saturday night got warped from *optional* nice-time-having into *obligatory* nice-time-having. And that the problem didn't stem from the Saturday night part as much as from the Imperative part.

Even when you coupled-up and got yourself a permanent date for Saturday night, you felt obliged to date up another couple. Think of the first years of marriage when someone called you on February 11 and invited you and your better half over for dinner for Saturday April 3. Remember how booked up in advance we all were during those young married days? How we spent hours at dinner parties with two or three other upwardly mobile dyads talking about issues and jobs and eating boned chicken breasts drowned in canned mushroom soup and sherry?

Those evenings were so organized, so forced, and so predictable that they felt just like having a Saturday night job. The job was to be convivial, conversational, clubby. And usually you were doing that with people you called your "friends" but who weren't really people you genuinely adored. They were just "The Martins" or the "The Raymonds," who came tidily packaged in twosomes and with whom you spent years of Saturday nights perfunctorily doing Saturday Night Things. But you weren't having a wonderful or a meaningful time. You were just Going Out.

Till you reached some subtle hey-wait-a-minute moment. And you recognized that with everyone's hectic work schedule, and accumulated depletion throughout the week, Saturday night was the one time you had to touch base with yourself and the few people you really cared for. That you just didn't have the energy or inclination for indiscriminate socializing, whether you were single or married. That you could afford to be selective. That you could afford to say no to regulation revelries and not qualify as a social leper. That the purest moments you had all week to nurture yourself were being wasted if you were sitting anywhere but where you really wanted to be.

And that Saturday isn't really the loneliest night of the week. It's only the last one. Or as my divorced friend, who was working real hard not to be depressed on Saturday nights, said, "I just wanted a Saturday night to pass and feel like any other evening. So I figured it really was only a Thursday coming two days late."

When It Happens
in Real Life

---

*T*he *Big Chill* was a lie.

When someone dies, and he's not supposed to, because he's your age—which is still young—and everyone reconvenes because you all need to be together to try and mute the horror, it becomes obvious that *The Big Chill* just couldn't happen.

You are all in too much pain. When someone dies at forty-four, and when you and everyone else who knew him way-back-when take planes in from all over so that within twenty-four hours you are all under the same roof, there is not one speck of energy left for anything other than raw anguish.

You are too depleted. Depleted by all the weeping, depleted by all the disbelief, depleted by all the despair. It is grief on a gargantuan scale laced with shock and rage and impotence. And, of course, occasional moments of laughter. Because you all have this fierce need to tell stories and remember the best times, this compulsion to get the great parts locked in permanently on the old memory disk. But unlike *The Big Chill*, there is room for no other drama, no nostalgic subplots.

In real life, when you all get together 'cause the pain is so bad, there is no rock and roll, no rekindling of old romances, no rehashing of old conflicts, and certainly no crawling into bed with your best friend's husband. In fact bed is the last thing on your mind at a time like this. You can't even sleep in it. Not when the waking up hurts so much.

So what you've got when someone forty-four years old gets taken out is a bunch of people with no skin on needing to be together again and yet realizing that they can never be together again because the person who made them feel the most together is never going to walk through that door. Which doesn't stop them from eyeing that door every couple of minutes and hoping against hope that he will come in and say, "Hey you guys, what's going on? How come you started without me?"

Of course the irony is we don't know how we are ever again going to start without him. How we're going to get up in the morning and face a world that doesn't have this man in it. Because he was no ordinary good guy. He happened to have been an extraordinary one. The kind who makes words like integrity and generosity and compassion kind of theadbare. The kind who makes you ask, why, with a world of jerks to pick from . . . and then you feel even more rotten for asking.

Questions when somebody this young dies have no answers anyway. Try looking for them. And all you see is a wife who has simply had her center blown away. And two kids who still have a lot of Dad conversations left that they're never going to have. And a mother whose soul has been savaged, because she has just completed the most unnatural act of all—she has just buried her only son.

That it has happened a million times, that it will happen a million more means nothing. It doesn't make you feel better, it doesn't make one thing easier, and it most definitely doesn't make a top-grossing film.

So *The Big Chill* was definitely Hollywood. Because in real life when you all get together again, because one of you has died about forty years too early, you are simply flattened. There is nothing there but naked heartache.

Yup, *The Big Chill* was only a movie. We should have known anyway. 'Cause in the movies, the good guys hardly ever die.

In memory of Bruce Siegel. April 2, 1943–January 25, 1988.

ON SEX
AND OTHER
BLUSHABLE
STUFF

Sexual Statistics

This month marks the fourth anniversary for the worst statistic ever foisted upon the unsuspecting American public.

It came from a *Ladies' Home Journal* readership survey and it has wreaked havoc with millions of marriages. Because here's what it said: It said that the average American woman makes love with her husband *three to five times a week.* Now the truth is that the average American woman barely has time to brush her teeth three to five times a week. Nonetheless, that statistic was taken by many as gospel. After all, *Ladies' Home Journal* is indeed a venerable publication. And while *Ladies' Home Journal* may stoop to air-brushing all of Angela Lansbury's wrinkles away when she appears on their cover, *Ladies' Home Journal* does not lie.

Thus, this is a statistic that has been making many of us feel crummy and substandard for years. Ladies at the grocery store still eye each other suspiciously, wondering if the exhausted working mom in front of them, shopping at 6:30 P.M. with one squalling kid in the basket and a briefcase full of homework, is actually one of the three-to-fivers. And men dragging home on the commuter train take a look at the other Willy Lomans and figure every last one of them is probably being greeted at the front door by a Saran-wrapped spouse holding a martini. So this statistic has done wonders for us: It has made millions of American women feel real inadequate and millions of American men feel real deprived.

Thus, it is with great pleasure that I now put an end to all that.

Because I have finally come across a piece of information that will really assuage those of us who do not quite measure up to the three-to-five-times-a-week category. It is a quote from an actual shrink. I found it in this month's *Vogue*, the periodical that I personally have always selected when I am seeking comfort and spiritual guidance. This is what the shrink, a Dr. Robert Shaw, who codirects the Family Institute of Berkeley, California, said:

[Some]thing that therapists know about relationships that I don't think the public knows is that if you are really sexually hot with someone, you are going to be different in so many dimensions that, in a certain way, you could say you're incompatible. It's almost inevitable that people who are extraordinarily attracted to each other are incompatible.

Now is that a great piece of information or what? Here, for all these years, you always thought the reason your libido just lay there like a lummox was all your fault: you always thought it was your problem that you were less exciting, less romantic, less willing to ignore the toenail clippings on the edge of the sink. But according to this doc, that isn't the deal at all. This doc says the reason you have hit the old sexual stalemate is simple—you get along. He's saying that in the Chinese restaurant of life, you actually only do get one from column A: You get peace, or you get passion. He's saying that the only way to be horny is to hate someone.

Three to five times a week, indeed.

Excuses, Excuses

Lest anyone think that The Big Guy sitting up there doesn't have a truly fab sense of humor, get a load of this little medical item: A neurology professor at Southern Illinois University reports that sex is one of the best cures for relieving a migraine headache. Especially if the sex takes place within the first thirty minutes after the onset of the headache.

Thus, the most acceptable excuse *not to have sex* known to mankind now bites the dust. Because instead of "Not tonight dear, I have a headache," we are going to soon be hearing . . . "Hurry up, dear, I have a headache."

Now that this piece of news is out you can rest assured that when somebody gets a headache, the first thing they reach for will *not* be the Tylenol.

Of course you know who will be having the headaches now, don't you? Let's just put it this way. It won't be the partner in the relationship who occasionally wears a skirt.

Obviously for the women of America, being robbed of the old reliable headache excuse poses an incredible challenge. It means that if you "aren't in the mood," you're going to have to come up with something a little more jaunty than your usual repertoire, which probably goes something like this:

1. It's too late.
2. It's too early.
3. Gary Hart is on "Nightline."

4. Ted Koppel is on "Nightline."
5. It's bad for my back.
6. It's bad for your back.
7. Sure. Just as soon as I finish getting my MBA.
8. The kids will hear.
9. The kids won't hear, but they'll know.
10. My nails are wet.
11. My nails are dry, but my toes are wet.
12. My toes are dry, but I forgot to put a top coat on my nails.
13. We just did it last month.

And for the men of America? Well, clearly it offers you the final revenge. After all these years, at long last, it will be *you* faking the headaches. Surely the irony of all this can't help but strike you as exquisite.

I know that sounds rather cynical. So I think we also should consider the brighter side—the huge improvement all this could be for the relationship between the sexes. For instance, think how much closer men and women will become through all this.

Look how much more we'll all have in common. How much more we'll share because of it. Because now with guys doing the same thing we always did, they'll understand just how we women felt all those years when we were faking headaches . . .

Not guilty at all.

Remember When It Was Only Tears on My Pillow?

Item: A London hotel is now offering its guests complimentary condoms instead of complimentary chocolates.

This is not good news for chocolate lovers.

This is also not good news for girls.

Consider the following scenario: Suppose you and Mr. Wonderful have just spent the longest evening on record wining and dining some customers. His customers. Your customers. No matter. The point is that for the past two hours you have been trapped in the hotel bar with some colossal yahoo and the Missus discussing the relative merits of polymers versus fibers. You are vastly bored and vastly tired. You would definitely like to be sound asleep up in your hotel room within the next three seconds. Finally, after many insincere good-byes, you and Mr. Wonderful ride the elevator up to the nineteenth floor, open the door, and are confronted with the sight of . . . A CONDOM ON THE PILLOW. Great. Just great.

A chocolate on the pillow is an amenity.

A condom on the pillow is a mandate.

A chocolate on the pillow is a courtesy.

A condom on the pillow is a command performance.

I mean there it sits. Blatantly mocking you. Blatantly telling you precisely what you are expected to do with the final segment of the evening.

This can get a girl to feeling just a tad pressured. I suppose, in all fairness, it can even get a guy to feeling a tad pressured. It's one thing if a condom is stashed with a bunch of other token toiletries in the amenity basket on the bathroom sink—that's what they do in Montreal's Shangrila Hotel. At least if it's tucked away in the basket, you can ignore it just like you ignore the sewing kit and shower cap.

However, their managing director says that 97 percent of the condoms they stash in the basket magically disappear the next morning. Of course M. Managing Director has no idea whether or not this is because they have been put to good use or because they represent something of a curio—after all the Shangrila is the first hotel in North America to offer complimentary condoms to its clientele.

But . . . Complimentary condoms are currently under serious discussion at the Hyatt chain. And you can just bet your complimentary mini-toothbrush that if Hyatt is discussing this, can Hilton and Marriott be far behind? The mind not only boggles, it blushes, and bemoans too.

Listen, I'm not opposed to safe sex. I'm not even opposed to sex. I just want it to feel like an option, not an obligation. But gee whiz. You walk into a room that has a condom sitting on the pillow and, well let's put it this way . . . how many of you have ever *not* eaten the chocolate?

Swim Your Way to Swell Sex

News Item: A recent study reveals that five hours of vigorous swimming can give those over forty the sex life of a twenty-year-old.

Comment: The first thing you might want to ask yourself after reading the above is: Who *wants* the sex life of a twenty-year-old? Consider what that tends to imply. No finesse, no seasoned moves, and a whole lot of time anguishing over the delicate issue of how to ask someone precisely where they have tested out on the old communicable-disease spectrum. In addition to which twenty-year-olds think it's real neat to make love on futons.

News Item Continued: According to this study, swimmers in their forties had sex 7.1 times a month. This is three times more than the average for forty-year-old nonswimmers.

Comment: Wait a minute. I'm not real swell in short division, but according to my trusty calculator, that would mean that nonswimming folks like you and I are only doing you-know-what 2.3 times a month. Most of us eat sushi more than that. I know we're supposedly old and I know we're supposedly bored, but gosh, 2.3 times a month sounds only slightly lustier than life around the neighborhood convent.

News Item Continued: There are several possible reasons that increased exercise leads to a more active sex life. Studies show that exercise brings about higher levels of the male hormone testosterone.

Comment: Studies also show that unusually high levels of tes-

YOU ONLY GET MARRIED FOR THE FIRST TIME ONCE

tosterone are found in men who are bald. Seems to me if you want to raise your testosterone levels it's a whole lot easier to go bald than to swim five hours a week.

News Item Continued: Another reason swimmers are sexually active is that they remain healthy enough to enjoy sex as they get older. This is because vigorous exercise improves heart and lung function.

Comment: I've always found that yelling was a good way to improve heart and lung function. And unlike swimming, when you're done yelling, you almost never need to blow-dry your hair.

News Item Continued: Swimming and sex are also likely to be linked, because people who swim are in great shape. Thus, they usually feel very good about their bodies and they are confident enough to pursue active sexual relationships.

Comment: Oh come on. Since when did anyone have to have a great body to pursue a sexual relationship? Why do you think Thomas Edison invented an off-switch for his little light bulb? Additionally, maybe swimmers are more active sexually simply because they've already taken the trouble to shave their legs and they might as well take full advantage of it.

And lastly, one is obliged to ask the big, industrial-strength philosophical question. I mean, considering that swimmers are so crazy about their own bodies, one can't help but wonder: When they are making love 7.1 times a month, just *whose body* are they *really* making love to, anyway?

Throb . . .
Throb . . .
Throb . . .

Remember when the raciest, horniest, most blush-instilling prose was made of words like "throbbing," "pulsating," and "ripe"? And they were always doled out judiciously amidst the dialogue that said stuff like "hurry, hurry" or "yes, yes" and just when you got to The Moment, you got . . . the old three dots every time. Those three dots packed enough mystery, eroticism, and sensuality to throw any self-respecting fourteen-year-old libido into overtime. God, those were the days when The Dirty Parts were really terrific.

As opposed to now. When The Dirty Parts are just—I don't know. Not even dirty. Just dopey. And about as close to erotic as Gene Shalit is to bald. Here's how I got to be such an authority on contemporary Dirty Parts. An adolescent I am related to called me into her room several years ago. "You've gotta hear this song by Prince." I generally undertake these sorties into the murky denizens of Her Music with great trepidation because I find it difficult to make a relevant remark about people with turquoise hair and zippered faces or songs on sentimental topics such as needing new drugs and the like.

But in this particular instance my interest was piqued. I'd been reading rave reviews about this Prince person's movie *Purple Rain*. So I figure, I can take in a few bars and maybe even emerge from the listening experience not only educated, but enthusiastic about the guy.

But tell me, how enthusiastic can you be about a guy who

sings something along the lines of actually wanting to f— the taste out of someone's mouth. Yes, folks. That is the very stuff our dewey-eyed teen darlings are listening to in their gingham-and-white eyelet and wicker rooms these days.

I, of course, hear it and scream. The adolescent and her visiting girlfriend are amused by this. They tell me to calm down, that it's the only Dirty Part. Dirty? This is not dirty. Bizarre maybe. Obscure maybe. Crude maybe. And confusing, definitely. I mean it's quite common to have lived a rich and full life in the sexual adventure department and never have encountered or even fantasized about encountering that particular phrase. But in terms of titillation, that quote hardly has the turn-on potential of a moan, a shudder, a "please, please," and the old dot dot dot deal.

And it begins to dawn on me. Our kids are being deprived of the great Dirty Parts. They think they've got it great, but all they've got is graphic. It's no fun anymore. It's just raw and raunchy. Take away the . . . and where is the mystery, the allure, the seduction?

God, was there anything juicier than being in ninth grade and getting hold of a contraband copy of *Peyton Place*? How many times in a row could you seethe and quiver through those Selena/Luke/Betty/Rodney/Constance/Tom couplings without having to go take a cold shower? Their writhings-on filled us with high hormonal wonderment. Even today, with all the f-words left out, and not a four-letter word for privates included, you cannot read page 277 of the hardcover edition without a rush.

And I wondered. How would a 1980s ninth-grader respond to page 277? How would your basic fourteen-year-old, who's crazy about Prince and has seen movies like *Fast Times at Ridgemont High*, in which sophomores are practicing oral-sex techniques on carrots, how would she react to page 277? Would she be impervious to the provocative possibilities of an "Again, darling, again," a "throb," a "quiver," and a few well-placed dots? Would she forever shatter her mother's vintage heart and toss the most widely read Dirty Parts book of the twentieth century aside, pronouncing it b-o-r-i-n-g? Or could her hormones be trained at this late date to stir at implicit lust rather than explicit lewdness? I casually left the book out and waited.

"Hey, Mom. This is pretty good. Do you mind if I read it?"

And I gave her precisely the same answer my mother gave to me when I wanted to read *Peyton Place* in the ninth grade. I didn't want to ruin her fun. I mean everyone knows what really makes the great dirty parts really dirty—Mommy won't let you see them. I told her "Not a chance."

Boy, was she in for a great time.

I Don't Do Thrill

Explain to me about roller coasters. Because I would rather be sent into any combat zone on the globe than take an assignment where my personal body would be topsy-turvy-ized, inverted, and whipped fiendishly about under the guise of wholesome, all-American fun-having.

What is fun about terror and throwing up? These are the only two responses I have ever experienced as the end result of a roller coaster ride. And for a long period in my life I felt these responses were indicative of a real character deficiency. I mean when you are fifteen years old and all you want in the world is for Vito Marzipone to think you are the swellest girl going, it is very hard to say no thank you when he takes you to Play 'n' Puke Park and says, "Ya wanna go on The Twister?" You would do almost anything (above the waist) for Vito Marzipone, but turning pewter gray, breaking out in a cold sweat, and heave-ho-ing it in the nearest trash bin seem an unlikely route for winning Vito's undying affections. The perverse appeal of these clackety contraptions totally escapes you, but at fifteen this is unthinkable.

But no more. Now I am convinced it is not moi who is deranged. It is all those crazed citizens who need to fill their kamikaze quotient by defying both God and gravity on one of those rickety rides. There apparently is some inexplicable charge they get in saying, "Come and get me" to the powers that be. This is called a "thrill." I don't do "thrill." I don't even get "thrill." I just get nauseous. I do not have to submit my stomach and my soul and my sweat glands to an interminable three minutes of cold white panic in order to feel joyous and grateful about being alive. I feel joyous and grateful about being alive when my checkbook balances.

But there are zillions of folks out there who require serious "thrill" in order to perk up their otherwise humdrum existence. Some choose to get it scrunching into a barrel and hurtling themselves over something moderately treacherous like Niagra Falls. Others, who perhaps have no access to barrels, or prefer to have their "thrill" dry, choose to do it by viewing tasteful cinematic offerings like *Son of Friday the Thirteenth Immolates the Second Cousin, Once Removed, of Indiana Jones*. Others simply ride the CTA.

But the need to ride some tottery engineering oddity called The Killer or The Comet or The Corkscrew, and have your stomach plastered all over your body, and operate under the conviction that this experience is FUN defies my comprehension. There is only one conviction a sensible person can hold when approaching a seventy-foot drop at a thirty-six-degree angle at a forty-five-mph cruising speed, and that is simply—you are gonna die.

Of course enthusiasts insist that coasters are Absolutely Safe and that what makes them so amusing is that you are not confronting *death*—you're just confronting *implied death*. Some of us fail to see the difference. They say what's so terrific about coasters is that for a few short minutes you are safely out of control. Perhaps. But sex accomplishes the same thing and for sex you don't have to wait in line. They say they love coasters because of the excruciating anticipation. But sex provides that too and unless you're with a real clod you get more than a thirty-five-second buildup. They say they love the intense rush that is absolutely legal. But sex gives you that, too, and when it's over you almost never toss your cookies.

My theory is that if you're looking for anticipation, abandon, and fun, sex does it a whole lot better than roller coasters. In fact the only advantage of roller coasters over sex is that they don't make you pregnant. Even I have to admit I'd rather ride a roller coaster once than have been Mrs. Vito Marzipone for life.

Cold Facts and
Hot Info

It was, as inappropriate questions go, quite swell.

"Mom, what is a vibrator?" This question was asked two thirds of the way through Sunday church services by an eleven-year-old boy.

The mom threw in an extra prayer, fixed him with a look that she hoped resembled enormous composure, and said, "Later."

The difference between that mom and many of us is that later she actually did fill the kid in. Because very few of our children seem to get the answers to these questions—or any sort of sexual info—from their moms and dads.

The interesting thing is that when a recent Harris Poll asked kids where they'd prefer to get their sexual information—from friends, school, or parents, nine out of ten said "Parents." That's the good news. The bad news is that, according to the same poll, the number who actually go to their parents for info is more like one out of ten.

You know why. We're afraid that sexual information may lead to sexual preoccupation. Or that too much candor about sex implies we're condoning sex. Or—and this is pretty hard to admit in the Dr. Ruth decade—plenty of us just don't want to talk about it because we are still *so* embarrassed.

It's true. Last spring when our local fifth grade was about to study human reproduction in school, parents were invited to preview the material their children would be viewing. A handful of moms showed up. And all of them—seasoned veterans as they obviously were of the birth process itself, or they wouldn't have been parents of fifth-grade kids—watched that filmstrip with considerable discomfort. They feigned calm, but every time some of the heavy-duty anatomical words and diagrams came up, there was lots of shifting in seats and body language that said, "Get me out of here."

Kids pick up on that. They don't come to us for information for two reasons. First of all, we're not so brilliant ourselves. A recent survey of American adults indicated that 96 percent have no idea how many days of each month a women can get pregnant (one day) and 94 percent have no idea how long a sperm lives (seventy-two hours). Both are rather salient biological points.

The second reason most kids don't come to us for info is this: Lots of us don't seem very "askable." If our kid pops up with a what-is-a-vibrator question we might choose to deflect it by asking "Where did you hear about those?" Or we might choose to ignore it. Or we might choose to laugh it off. But my God, we would rather do almost anything than answer it.

So we've got to keep working on becoming a lot more askable.

Because if we don't become askable, you know what we become don't you? We become very young grandparents.

But You Forgot
My Pinch

Everybody has one or two questions they just hate having people ask them. Stuff they are kind of sensitive about.

Usually people ask us these questions intending no malice. They just ask us these questions sort of conversationally. They have no idea that, for us, this is a killer question. One that thrusts a little tiny lance into our hearts.

This is exactly what happened to me the other day. I'm sure that when this person posed this question to me, he expected a simple, perhaps even amusing, response. He must have been rather surprised then to find my little eyes tearing up, my little voice aquiver, and my little soul so obviously disassembled.

Here's the question: "When you lived in Italy, did you get pinched and hassled by men a lot?"

This is not a mean question. And it's also a perfectly logical question to ask a woman who lived in Italy for three years and who just returned from visiting there. Perfectly logical. What was not logical was the shame, self-loathing, and general despair that coursed through me when I had to tell him my answer. My answer was, "No. Not even once."

I realize that this answer qualifies me for Ripley's Believe It Or Not. This does not make me happy. I would prefer not to be the only woman in the world who walked around for approximately one thousand days on Italian soil without eliciting one turned head, one oily invitation, one perfunctory pinch. I know that from a feminist standpoint my sense of deprivation is reprehensible. But that is precisely how I feel despite being a member of NOW, a charter subscriber to *Ms. Magazine,* and a woman with all my credit cards in my own name. Life is full of little dichotomies.

I am not proud of wanting to pinched. I am not even sure I really wanted it. I simply expected it. I simply expected to be able to roll my eyes like every other woman who has ever been to Italy and sigh with great exasperation, "God, these men, they never leave you alone."

Only they did. For three entire years.

Ultimately I think I figured out why. Or at least I rationalized why. The entire time I lived in Rome, I was either highly pregnant or pushing an occupied stroller. It became clear that as long as I was bambino-laden, there was no way an Italian man considered me fair game. They take their madonnas very seriously over there.

Which was why I was so ecstatic when I returned to Rome last month. This time I was sure I'd finally get my pinch. The bambinos are big now, and while I'm not pushing any strollers, no one's pushing me in a wheelchair. I still should be capable of eliciting some lacivious Latin responses.

Nothing the first day, nothing the second, nothing the third. But on the fourth day, I was strolling along the Via Condotti with one of the kids, and finally it came. A guy with absolutely no room in his pants to even slip in a dime smiled appreciatively and turned to his friend to say, "Now that one, that one is really something."

My heart fluttered. My spirits soared. My ego inflated. It wasn't a pinch, but it was almost as good. For one brief shining moment I was euphoric. Until I heard what his friend said.

"Yeah, too bad she's with her mother."

Not My Mom and Dad

How's this for nifty kid-raising advice: It is perfectly fine to close the bedroom door and tell the kids, "Daddy and I want to be alone now, we're going to make love."

Now that you're back up off the floor, I will tell you that this pearl of wisdom was offered by an actual nurse who just wrote an actual book on this.

The book suggests that parents do this "to reinforce the concept that parents have sexual feelings and make love for pleasure."

Oh come on. Everybody knows parents don't Do It. The only times they ever Did It are the two times they Had To when they wanted to have you and your brother. You are forty years old and you still believe this. I mean you are perfectly willing to accept that other people's parents might have Done It recreationally, but by some bizarre biological Ripley's Believe It Or Not coincidence, you KNOW that you are the only kid in the world (except your brother) whose parents only Did It twice.

Kids, even when they are forty, do not like to be confronted with their parents' sexuality. There is a very profound reason for that. This is the profound reason: It's just SO EMBARRASSING.

Also, it is important for every generation to feel that they, and they alone, have discovered sex. There is no point in even indulging in sex if you think your parents were doing it, because as everyone knows, anything our parents ever did or thought was totally dumb and totally irrelevant. Lust just wouldn't be any fun at all if we hadn't been lucky enough to have invented it.

But let's talk some more about embarrassment. Given the choice between embarrassment and enlightenment, most of us will take embarrassment every time. Kids should not be enlightened about sex. If they're enlightened about sex they will never say perfectly adorable things that you can bore all your friends with like, "The egg and the squirm meet and fight it out. If the egg wins, it's a girl. If the squirm wins, it's a boy. The bossier one wins." Darling, wouldn't you much rather hear them say that than something like, "Mom and Dad are in the bedroom now making love, which is both a natural biological and emotional function of a close committed relationship."

Anyway, that wouldn't be their response. In fact, when asked how they would feel if their parents told them they were going in the bedroom to make love, a random survey of three children, age nine to fourteen, responded thusly:

Random Child #1—"Rude!"

Random Child #2—"Gross!"

Random Child #3—"That's the most disgusting thing I've ever heard!"

We might also point out that it's not just a question of the little ones being fully awake and fully aware of what's going on behind the bedroom door. It's also a question of your knowing that they're on the other side of the bedroom door fully awake and fully aware. It would be unlikely in such an instance that anyone on either side of that bedroom door would be having what is referred to as "a quality time."

In any case, it is clear that telling your kids you are about to Do It is a colossally dopey idea. Because hard as it is to imagine your saying it, and hard as it is to imagine your kid dealing with your saying it, it is even harder to imagine one other thing.

What in the world would you say when you opened the bedroom door and came out?

The Return of the Hickey

At first I didn't know what to make of it.

I mean it IS 1988, right? and the woman, a respected TV producer, HAD to be in her mid-thirties, right?

But there it was. The telltale purple red splotch. Incontrovertible evidence, incongruous evidence, and incredible evidence—the woman had a hickey!

Now I know how shocked you are. Actually you are probably shocked on two levels. Level number one must be your fundamental astonishment at the existence today, on the neck of a full-fledged adult, of such a total anachronism as a hickey, or lovebite, or whatever they called it in your high school. Level two must be your fundamental astonishment that we are actually *talking about* the existence of a hickey, no matter whose neck it's on.

However I have always tried to examine both the profundities and the minutiae of life. And to point out the irrevocable connection between the two.

Not to mention . . . *trends*. And what concerns me about this hickey is not only that it might be a trend, but that it actually is one of those seeming scraps of minutiae that might be rife with a profundity. Bear with me a moment.

Let's talk about days of yore. I mean real yore, like when we were sixteen and girls spent hours worrying about How Far to Go and not be considered a sleaze or—even worse—a tease, and boys spent hours figuring how to swoop their arm around a girl in the movies and let it dangle nonchalantly where it wasn't supposed to be. That yore.

Hickeys were a very integral part of all that. And in a sense they were sort of a red badge of courage, a signal, that you were wild, but not That Wild. If you were That Wild, you would have been doing something else besides wasting your time biting each other's necks. Hickeys are like PG-13 movies. You think they're pretty hot stuff after being limited to G and PG, but you never bother with them once you're seriously into R.

And there were a lot of theories about hickeys. Like how to give them . . . overtly, which involved a borderline Dracula imitation. Or covertly, which required that the giv-ees be both speedy and subtle so that the get-ees had a major surprise awaiting when they put on their V-neck sweaters the next morning. Of course by the time you'd refined your technique, you were usually ready to jump to the serious stuff and hickeys became moot. And I figured they were pretty much moot ever since.

But then along came the 1980s. When sex got very dangerous. When herpes made it scary and AIDS made it lethal. When surveys indicated that the number one fear of women today isn't nuclear war or cancer or poverty—it's STD—sexually transmitted diseases.

So I think that's what I saw on the TV producer's neck. The modern woman's response to STD. That hickey was one giant step backward into the world of safe sex. Only instead of being a red badge of courage as it once was in high school, in the grown-up world it's a red badge of terror.

How's your supply of turtlenecks?

Passion Places

Go ahead and tell me I've got a dirty mind. But suppose you saw this scenario . . .

It's a small, decrepit post office. A plain, harried-looking woman, in her mid-thirties, pulls up in her burgandy Buick. In the back, there is a toddler jammed into a kiddie seat. Defying all rules of parental common sense, she leaves the kid in the car while she charges into the post office lobby.

Her hand (with wedding ring) is shaking as she inserts a key into box 158. A look of intense euphoria crosses her face. She pulls out a small white envelope. She waits not one second to rip it open. And then, in a parked vehicle, with the kid starting to squall, she begins to read, smile, stare off into space, and to reread the postal missive she has just received.

So what do you think is going on? 1) Ed McMahon has just written her that she won the Publishers Clearing House Sweepstakes. 2) She just got a good report card from a Draw Me correspondence course. 3) This lady is having an affair. Come on folks. You know the answer. Definitely numero three. No one rents a post office box unless they are seriously into the plain brown wrapper syndrome or having a torrid affair.

I present this scenario to point out to those who indulge in these sordid goings-on that there are more places than just motels that are dead giveaways. Places that are seemingly benign beyond belief actually reek of illicit liaisons to those of us who are astute social observers. For instance:

The 7-Eleven. Without question, the 7-Eleven is a veritable mecca for the adulterers of America. That's because it offers an unbeatable array of attractions. It is always open, so it offers a lot of accessibility. It always has telephones, so it offers a lot of allure. It always has cigarettes, so it offers wonderful alibis.

The Zoo. Talk about blowing the whistle. Anytime you see a stylishly dressed man and woman sitting on a park bench on a Tuesday afternoon, you know they are up to no good. This is particularly evident if one of the stylishly dressed duo is crying.

The Beach in Any Season but Summer. Now this is axiomatic. Two people seen either sitting or walking along the beach are never, I repeat, NEVER, discussing anything harmless. Ever since time immemorial, ever since *From Here to Eternity*, ever since Frankie and Annette, it has been very clear that beaches are second only to beds when it comes to non-innocent environments.

The Pay Phone Down the Street. Really, this looks extremely shabby. When I pass our neighborhood pay phone on a Sunday afternoon and see a woman who lives four houses away, who has a minimum of two telephone lines in her house, speaking furtively into the mouthpiece, what am I to presume? That she's planning a surprise party for her husband???

I know, I know. Evil is in the eye of the beholder. But tell the truth. It kind of makes you wonder why your honey has been so willing to go to the all-night laundromat lately, doesn't it?

The Big "O" and the Big $

This has to be the ultimate blow. According to a recent survey, *51 percent of American women think about money more often than sex. And nearly one third of them ENJOY money more than sex.*

Men tend to disagree, traditionalists that they are. They still think whoopee is considerably sweller than wampum.

But women seem to have arrived at the point where The Big "O" has been replaced by the Big $. And I guess if you think about it, you can sort of see why.

First of all, money is about the only topic left that is considered absolutely private. I mean there's intimacy and there's intimacy. It's one thing to share your body with someone, it's quite another to share your bankbook. Here is a test. Start counting on one hand the number of people with whom you've shared the former. Did you run out of fingers? Now start counting on the other hand the number of people with whom you've shared the latter. I think you get the drift.

In an age where the modern woman can discuss erogenous zones, positions preferred, and fantasies she has indulged in without batting an eyelash, money remains the last indelicate subject. Not only is it indelicate, it's actually almost vulgar. No wonder she thinks about it all the time.

And . . . money still reeks of mystery. There's no mystery about sex anymore. There's not even any guilt. Darling Dr. Ruth took care of that. So what fun is sex if you can't feel rotten about it afterward?

But money is still deliciously drenched in guilt. It's perfectly possible for a woman to sleep with two men at one time and not give it a thought. But it is constitutionally impossible for that same woman to see a $200 pair of leather boots and buy them without major trepidation and kilos of anguish. Even if she can afford them. Of course money's biggest contribution in the guilt department is the old if-I-stay-home-will-we-be-able-to-buy-the-kids-new-tennis-shoes-twice-a-year versus if-I-work-will-they-grow-up-to-be-normal-human-beings-capable-of-taking-nourishment-in-public-restaurants-without-drooling dilemma. It's really quite the exquisite contemporary quandry.

So it's no wonder that women are thinking about money more than sex. Money is still very private, very mysterious, a tad vulgar, and absolutely laced with horrendous feelings of guilt. Sex at this point offers none of the above.

Poor sex. It has really taken a beating from us ladies this year. Remember a few years back when Ann Landers announced that 90,000 of her female readers overwhelmingly preferred hugs to sex? Well perhaps the question should be posed again. Only now that we know sex isn't number one on any woman's list, perhaps we should ask the pivotal question: What would you rather have—lots of hugs or lots of money?

One shudders to think of the response.

So Long, Smooching

It's just possible that the eighties may go down in history as the decade kissing became extinct. God knows it's been on the wane in most adult lives for long enough.

Oh there's still some kissing going on. But most of it falls in these three categories. 1) The medicinal kiss. This is the one which has healed the boo-boos of trillions of toddlers since time immemorial. 2) The social kiss. This is the one where you say, "Darling, you look terrific" and then kiss directly into the air immediately to the right or left of the other person's cheek. 3) The hand kiss. This doesn't happen real often unless you happen to hang out with Ricardo Montalban a lot.

But as for real kissing . . . Discounting the times when you are naked and horizontal in bed, when was the last time you were engaged in one of those great smoochy heart-racers we all used to do for hours on end, till our mouths were numb, and our cheeks were scraped, and our car windows were thoroughly fogged over?

Truth is, once you and your honey have been together for a few years, the only kissing that's going on are those perfunctory little hello and good-bye ones. And most of us don't even do that. We tend instead to just embrace and sort of pat each other on the back—you know, the marital burp syndrome.

In fact, most of us would have thought that serious kissing had already gone the way of the dinosaurs if it had not been for the movies and TV. But you could always turn on the tube at eleven in the morning any weekday and find some lady in a gold lamé ensemble clutched in a slurpy, suctiony salutation with some gentleman caller.

Only no more. Now, actors and actresses are refusing to play any scenes in which they are involved in lusty, open-mouth kissing. It's part of the AIDS scare. Which, while intellectually understandable, is truly distressing when you consider the inspirational role models movie kisses have always been.

From the very first one, they have set the standards for great smooching. The first movie kiss, filmed in Thomas Edison's studio in 1896, was exchanged by a Miss May Irwin and a Mr. John Rice for the film *The Widow Jones*. This kiss was apparently so terrific that it inspired the first demand for movie censorship. It probably also inspired a lot of 1896 kids, as yet uninitiated in the intricacies of steamy kissing.

One can only imagine how the young swains of the twenties could have managed without Valentino to guide them, or the young swains of the forties without Errol Flynn to guide them, or the young swains of the early sixties without Troy Donahue to guide them. (Well you saw what happened in the sixties.) When you're experimenting on your pillow or the back of your hand, it's very hard to nail down the moves when you can't practice what you've seen in the movies.

And now we're going to be left with no inspiration at all. The only kisses we'll see will be white bread, locked-lipped Brady Bunch ones. Which hardly gets that old black magic running up and down your spine. Yes indeed, the eighties could be a bad decade for kissing.

It's enough to turn you into an Eskimo.

Is There Sex After Divorce?

The question these days isn't "Is there sex after marriage?" The question is "Is there sex after divorce?"

Most of us think that one of the major activities of the recently uncoupled is constant coupling. We see divorced people as participants in randy Dionysian revels while we remain stuck in the quagmire of meatloaf and gray jockey-shorts domesticity. Well, according to those who are indeed out there on the cutting edge of recently acquired single-dom, life among the great dee-vorced is far from sybaritic. The problem as described by Nan, who like all recently divorced females went right out and bought pounds of frilly underwear, is that she is all undressed with no place to go.

Because now men have custody too. In days of yore there used to be sleek chocolate-brown studio apartments filled with divorced dads who had waterbeds and stereos, and visitation rights on weekends. This is no longer the case. Now dads rent places that are less swell, but more spacious. And they don't furnish their bedrooms with seductive products. They furnish them with the products of their previous seductions—their kids.

Nan says post-divorce sex is about as logistically convoluted to pull off as premarital sex used to be. Only instead of having to circumnavigate everybody's parents, you're constantly trying to circumnavigate everybody's kids. (Except in the case of Michael, a well-to-do divorced lawyer, who being a good Jewish son, lets his mother stay the winter in his Florida condo. Which means that

Michael, who pays a sizable monthly maintenance on his $150,000 abode, finds himself renting $39.95 Tampa motel rooms so he can get a little time alone with his lady friend. God forbid his mother should know that her fifty-year-old son is actually engaging in sex *without the sanctity of marriage.)*

Without the sanctity of marriage is the pivotal issue here. Married people are dodging the kids, too, but at a certain point (like when the kids start staying up later than you do), you can close the bedroom door, because ultimately kids can deal with the concept that—disgusting as it may seem—Mom and Dad probably do Do It. Once a year.

But Mom and A DATE and a closed bedroom door is a concept a whole lot thornier to deal with. Same thing with Dad and A DATE. Thus, we find that men who are paying their ex-wives for one bedroom they no longer sleep in, and paying their own rent for another that they do, have to pay for a third in order to get a little nooky back in their life.

According to Nan, there are a surprising number of divorced doctor/lawyer/merchant-chief types pulling down six-figure incomes who have accrued a vast knowledge of $15-for-three-hour motels. And while this sounds sort of steamily glamorous to those of us still firmly ensconced in monotony of marital bliss, Nan assures me that it wears thin real fast. That after the theater or a lovely dinner, two otherwise respectable single parents would prefer to fall into bed somewhere that did not reek from the revels of others.

But the options are limited. Of course there's always the car. Nan acknowledges that not only has she defiled every inch of her own car, but that she has left footprints on the ceilings of others.

It does give one pause. Married sex may occasionally seem like a chore, but at least it doesn't require the added chore of first cleaning off the backseat of the Chevy.

GUY
NOTES

Can the Maternity Jockstrap Be Far Behind?

Male pregnancy. Is that music to a woman's ears, or what?

Well, guess what girls—according to *Omni* magazine, male pregnancy is going to be a real option in only ten or twenty years. The recipe is pretty simple: Take one test-tube embryo the size of a needle tip, implant it on the large intestine, the placenta will develop and nurture the fetus, and nine months later wheel the guy into the delivery room for one of the gynecologists' favorites, the ever-popular cesarean operation. Yes indeed. At last it will be possible for men to enjoy the exquisite experience of giving birth. An experience they've thus far been denied.

The problem is, your average male may be a bit hesitant to take advantage of the pregnancy option. In fact, here are the responses of several average males when asked how they would feel about becoming pregnant:

"As long as the mother would marry me, it would be okay."

"Do I have to?"

"I think I'm busy that day. Maybe we could just have lunch."

"It just wouldn't feel right."

What these guys don't know from feeling right. Although Groucho once said having babies was easy enough to imagine: "Just take hold of your lips—now fold them back over your head."

Thus, once the male pregnancy option becomes a biological possibility, we women may still have to do a bit of convincing to get our men prepared for the leading role in what has been called (heh

heh) "the miracle of birth." Therefore, in preparation for this big birthtech breakthrough, let us explain to you men some of the far-reaching benefits pregnancy will offer you.

First of all, it will become your ultimate bargaining chip. We all know the seriousness with which the modern couple divvies up the domestic duties along 50-50 lines. I do the marketing, you do the cooking, I do the garbage, you do the fish tank, etc. It now will be possible to really scale up the ante. I would venture that an "I'll do the pregnancy" offer on the part of any man, could garner you at least thirty to forty years of folded socks *and* ironed underwear. With no bitching.

Secondly you've got your cataclysmic mood swings. Pregnancy will offer you a wonderful nine-month opportunity to weep at the drop of a hat, kvetch constantly, and have trillions of temper tantrums. (We of course will do our best not to be too patronizing and blame the whole thing on your hormones.)

Speaking of hormones, as a pregnant man, you will have to understand if, during this time, your wife seems to be considerably more interested in sex than you are (beast that she is). Not to worry. Just tell her that the doctor said is isn't safe. That one has been working for years.

One of the things you will probably enjoy most during your nine months is the chance to gorge without guilt. Remember you are eating for two. Even though one of you is the size of a pinhead and the other of you is rapidly becoming the size of Trump Tower. Not to worry, the body accommodates all this. Why else do you think God invented stretch marks and varicose veins? Little badges of your biological valor that you can carry with you for life.

Additionally, pregnancy offers you a wonderful chance to believe in Tinker Bell, Santa Claus, all things bright and beautiful again. What we mean by this is you will not once, during this time, ever hear the word "pain" mentioned. Nor will you hear the term "excruciating pain." You will never hear the words "moaning" or "writhing." Pregnancy will afford you a wondrous journey back into the world of fantasy.

I have saved the best for last. By far, the most lasting benefit you men will gain from your pregnancy is humility. Let me assure you there is nothing quite like birthing a baby to knock any egotistical notions right out of you. There you'll be—flat on your back, knees raised, sheets covering you everywhere but where you long to be covered, with only four nurses, a doctor, an anesthesiologist, a resident, and four thousand medical students from Third World countries in attendance. But don't worry. Your wife will be with you, too.

She'll be the one with the video camera.

Mirror, Mirror . . .

I cling very tenaciously to the belief that there is no room in a relationship for two people with blow dryers. I like my men unvarnished. A hot shower, a good shave, and a shot of mouthwash is about all the male artifice and dandification I'm programmed to deal with gracefully.

So initially I attributed my abhorrence of men's moisturizer, astringent, and night creams to my base sexist nature. I was a female chauvinist pig. Oink. Oink. But I'm beginning to think my antipathy for the preening, vainglorious gent is actually based on something more substantive than my retro rats 'n' snails 'n' puppie dog tails perception of the male species. It's based on sadness.

It's beginning to occur to me as I watch the sales figures mount at male cosmetic counters for toners, bronzers, and facial masks that the exact opposite of what we thought all this was supposed to indicate is actually going on. What we thought was going on was that the contemporary man had become so liberated that he could cross over into a formerly all-female domain and treat himself to a bit of cosmetic indulgence.

But what's really going on isn't a sign of liberation at all. It's actually a sign of entrapment. These guys are buying into the same trap that we have been buying into for years: namely that looking good is mightily important. Important enough to spend lots of dollars and lots of hours in front of the mirror preening, and pruning, and painting. And that somehow there is a definite link between how small your pores are or how thick your hair looks and how you are valued as a human being.

This is precisely the viewpoint that women have been toiling to decimate for the last two screaming, strident, sermonizing decades. But most of us still put on mascara, still check the mirror daily to see who's winning the wrinkles versus collagen race, and still pull out the lipstick after dinner in a restaurant just in case we run into Robert Redford on our way out to the car. We still are, if truth be told, a little pathetic.

And now the guys get to be a little pathetic too. I remember, last spring, standing under an awning for twenty minutes with two friends because it was drizzling outside. The woman and I were willing to walk back to our offices, but her husband had just had his hair done at a chi-chi hair salon, and didn't want to risk it. So much for the liberated man.

So much for the liberated woman, too. We thought that by stepping into the working world liberation was ours. Only we made the same mistake the men are making at the cosmetic counter. We're taking it all too seriously. And by doing so, instead of being liberated by our careers, we're getting trapped in the mindset that has haunted men for years. Suddenly we're beginning to measure our worth as human beings by the number of zeros on our paychecks and the number of windows in our offices.

So instead of culling the best from each other's domains, we've taken the worst. Now we're never going to know if men love us for ourselves or for our five-figure incomes. And men are never going to know if we love them for themselves . . . . or for their flawless complexions.

Guys 'n' Dolls

It was a word I hadn't heard in decades.

"So long, *doll*," said my man-friend.

I hung up the phone with a huge cheshire act grin. *Doll.* Boy did it ever feel great to hear someone say that again. Not only to hear it, but to like it. And to admit to liking it. Not to see it as some deprecatory dismissal by a male chauvinist oink-oink, but to be able to accept it as it was intended. As light, as affectionate, as . . . nice.

Truth is, we've made it real hard for guys to say things like that for a long time. Terms of endearment have become rather dicey territory in boy/girl banter. Oops. Man/Woman banter.

That's another thing. There is no such word as "girl" these days. Not even when you're still a girl. Ask any eleven-year-old female. We're all "women." The only people who still say "girl" are the sixty- and seventy-year-olds who invite the "girls" over for bridge. Apparently most of us women just aren't old enough to be "girls." But I digress . . .

The point is, guys (whom we still get to call "guys" even though they would have to be hospitalized if they attempted to call us "gals") have become somewhat tongue-tied in the past couple of decades when it came to calling us something nice and breezy and warm. Like "doll." Any man who tried to call a woman "doll" in the past decade risked serious dismemberment, and you know which member I mean.

Because just like Rodney Dangerfield, and just like Aretha Franklin, we wanted RESPECT. Which is definitely a good thing, and something no woman should ever be without. But we got so hung up on it. So adamant. That sometimes we forgot to notice when we already had it. Our dukes were up and there was no one to fight.

A whole lot of men out there not only respect women. They adore them, too. And while we're delighted with their respect, we're still a bit skittish when it comes to dealing with their adoration. We sometimes feel that the latter can't help but undermine the former. Big mistake.

My man-friend is no oink-oink. He single-daddied a couple of kids all the way into college. He scours copper bottoms with the best of them. And he makes a mean turkey tetrazzini. So who else is more entitled to hand me my first "doll" in ten years?

And me? I don't want to get too self-congratulatory here, but it seems to me that just possibly the mark of an ultimately liberated, well-adjusted woman might be the ability to have someone she genuinely likes call her "doll" and not get all bent out of shape about is. To stop being so defensive. And to let her heart get warmed by it and to know that it's meant as a lovely verbal hug.

And not a four-letter word.

Selective
Honorability

Eleven-thirty A.M. Charlie's off to a convention in New Orleans. First thing he does when he gets to the airport is buy himself a pack of cigarettes. He "quit" three months ago, which means he doesn't smoke at home where the fitness-crazed wife and kids can nail him, and he doesn't smoke in the office where the upward-bound exec is supposed to look habit-free. But this is New Orleans, and hell, one pack isn't going to hurt.

Two-thirty P.M. Charlie's got a great cabbie taking him to the hotel. The guy really knows the city and is giving him names of a couple of not-to-be-missed jazz clubs. Terrific guy. When Charlie asks for a receipt the guy says, "Sure. Here ya' go. In fact here are a couple extra blank ones." Charlie takes them. Those can come in mighty handy when you're filling out the old expense report.

Four-thirty P.M. The booth in the exhibition hall checks out fine. So with the rest of the afternoon free, Charlie decides to go shopping. While picking up a few gifts for the family, he spots an absolutely sensational suitcase. The price is outrageous. The wife would be appalled. Not just to find it on her Visa bill at the end of the month, but just to know that he was willing to pay that much for the suitcase. But Charlie really wants that suitcase. So he pays for it with cash. He'll just tell her it cost less. That way she won't feel so bad.

Eleven P.M. It's been an interesting evening. An attractive woman sales rep from Detroit has been very friendly and she, Charlie, and several others are just heading back from dinner. Someone proposes that they all go up to the bar for one last drink. Charlie would like to have a drink with her alone just to get to know her better. She says she'd really like that, but it's a bit awkward with everyone there tonight and maybe tomorrow night they can "work something out." Charlie likes how that sounds.

Eleven-thirty A.M. It's the next day. Charlie has cut out of the convention for a while. And in the middle of his sight-seeing, he remembers a call he has to make. When he's all done, he hangs up the pay phone and starts to cross the street. And then—a nasty little chastisement . . . RINGGGGGG. Ma Bell is ticked. She's demanding more silver.

Charlie stops dead in the middle of the street. Not a soul is around. Ma Bell could jangle and bluster and rage for hours and no one one would ever be the wiser if Charlie walked off into the sunset. There's no witness, no way to trace him. For a moment Charlie is paralyzed. Feels like he's face to face with his maker. It's quite the pivotal moment.

And it's the moment he tells his kids all about when he gets home from his trip. He tells them the story of the pay phone jangling on the empty street, and he makes sure that they understand *why* Daddy walked back across the street to put that quarter in the phone. Because he *had* to, he tells them with great gravity.

Otherwise it would have been cheating.

Baby-Sitter Banter

It's hard to believe in 1988 that there is actually a Social Problem for Male Persons that is so embarrassing no one has yet had the nerve to address it. It has been avoided in books, ignored in advice columns, and absolutely neglected by TV.

However, in our continuing effort to confront the thornier questions of contemporary life, we will now, for the first time in a public forum, address this pressing issue: WHAT DOES A MALE PERSON SAY TO A BABY-SITTER WHILE DRIVING THIS BABY-SITTER HOME?

The reason this poses a problem is, 1) in a two-parent household, no matter how liberated, male persons are usually the persons stuck with baby-sitter pickup and delivery duty; 2) male persons are very non-good at small talk.

In their defense, it must be said that small talk, for anyone, is especially hard with a teenager. Actually large talk is also hard with a teenager. It is even hard for the adults who are actually related to that teenager. But for a nonrelative, who is also a male person, trying to find a suitable topic to get you through a five-minute drive makes locating the Holy Grail seem like a piece of cake.

No subject works. Especially the obvious one. Such as The Children. Ask them how the kids were and all you're going to get is "Okay." No rave reviews. And no candid complaints. No fourteen-year-old is going to say, "You got yourself a real monster there, Mr. Farqwart." They're not stupid. They know who's paying them two bucks an hour to sit in front of the video cassette and devour all the Dove Bars.

Nor is the subject of their higher education particularly inspirational. Ask them "How's school?" and, whether they are president of the student body or the record holder for suspensions, you'll get the same answer—"Okay." Which pretty much wraps that one up.

Of course the real mistake is to ask something specific. Like, "Do you go out for any sports?" This is perceived by a baby-sitter as an Incredibly Embarrassing Question. It is perceived as Too Personal. Questions like that are considered about one step removed from making a pass.

Thus, unless you resort to asking baby-sitters how they feel about the federal deficit, the conversational options are fairly well exhausted by the time you have pulled out of the driveway. And you will find yourself, whether you are a person who has argued in front of the Supreme Court, lectured in front of thousands of university students, or interviewed hundreds of candidates for important career posts, thoroughly intimidated by a fourteen-year-old monosyllabic being. It's a stunning moment of awkwardness.

There is of course only one solution. Give up. Realize that conversation is only possible when the participants have something in common. So turn up the radio and sit in the car and don't talk.

Just like you do with your wife.

Lawn Envy

If you happen to be a guy person, listen up.

Because there's a new development on the old scientific horizon that's going to CHANGE YOUR LIFE FOREVER. According to the reknowned scientific journal *People* magazine, some guy has invented a grass that doesn't need to be watered, that doesn't need to be fertilized, and that only needs to be mowed once a year.

Now on the surface, this probably sounds like real good news. But the truth is, an invention like this could wreck a guy's weekend or even a guy's life (one's life and one's weekend being for many guy persons somewhat interchangeable).

I mean just imagine. Just imagine an entire weekend without having to mow a lawn. It's practically un-American. Lawn mowing is what an American guy does in between sports events. What's he gonna do now? Read a little Proust?

Come on. A lawn is not just a lawn. A lawn represents many unspoken things to the average American guy. It says, "I am the all-American citizen." It says, "I am the all-American provider." It says, "I am the all-American nurturer." And most all-American of all, it says, "Mine is bigger and better than yours."

Now, no PhD.s have been done on this yet, but "lawn envy" is one of the great unexplored domains of the male psyche. For some as yet undocumented reason, a lot of guys feel their self-worth is directly related to the texture, tone, and critter-free-ness of their front lawn.

A man can deal with a wife who betrays him—if he can go on Oprah's infidelity show.

A man can deal with a body that betrays him—if he can go on Donahue's impotence show.

But a man can not deal with a lawn that betrays him—that is just too sensitive an arena, too hot a topic. Even Oprah and Phil won't touch it.

So take away lawns as the ultimate barometer by which men judge each other, and what pray tell is going to happen to a pivotal aspect of American life?

Not to mention a pivotal aspect of American marriage. Now no one likes to talk about this too much, but have you ever noticed what a divorced woman's lawn looks like? N.G.—Not Good, at all. Actually, you can drive down any block in America and just by looking at the lawns get a pretty clear idea of the marital status of the women inside. Indeed it's a well-known fact that many a woman has stayed married to many a man just because she can't bear to deal with the grass.

In fact, as my friend Renee said just yesterday about Mr. Renee. "Sometimes I could just kill him. But I'll probably never unload him. I tell you, Harvey gives great lawn."

And now comes this no-mow/no-water grass.

So long, Harvey.

Cars Do Not the Man Make

Here's a little something that should make every man in America feel a bit better. It's about this notion you guys have that sporty, snappy, sassy cars are a major attribute when it comes to attracting wonderful women. I think you should know something. "Car" has never been on the list of the top fifty criteria when it comes to rating a male person's attractiveness. Not if the list is being done by someone with more than a double-digit IQ.

I wonder when you guys came up with this notion. It's not like it's well-rooted in history. God knows no self-respecting cowboy ever figured a four-on-the-floor palomino would help him to lure in the Miss Kittys. And I'm sure no self-respecting pharaoh ever counted on his two-tone camel to win the heart of his local Cleopatra. But somewhere along the way, men began to attribute wonderful seductive powers to the make and model of their mode of transport.

I know this because last week my husband, a man who has never driven anything more exotic than a beige Reliant, came in waving an article that, he said, "was the best thing I've ever read on how men feel about cars." I've lived with this man two decades and didn't know he'd ever had any feelings about cars other than wanting them to go chug-chug when he turned the key and put his little foot on the pedal.

This article absolutely waxed rhapsodic about what a great car could do for the male ego. The gist of all this poetry was that any man who wrapped himself in a Corvette suddenly assumed the swellness of Mel Gibson. Oh, silly silly man. The situation is absolutely AU CONTRAIRE.

I have been surveying women for one straight week on this issue. Not one woman surveyed had ever, once she had abandoned her pom-pom phase, grown all melty over a guy because he pulled up in a certain kind of car. There was one case in which a respondent theorized that if a guy came to pick her up and the fender of his vehicle clanged to the ground, it's probably unlikely that she would be enchanted. But beyond that, there was absolutely no connection between Plymouths, Porsches, and passion.

In fact (and here comes the AU CONTRAIRE part), a significant chunk of women grow very suspicious when they see that a man is tooling around in a car that costs $40,000 or more. Women see a man in one of those, and they get to wondering. Because no matter how rich someone is, unless his last name is Rothschild, $40,000 is an enormous percentage of his annual income. Women get to wondering what type of person is so needy of feeling like ole Mel that he would be willing to put that kind of money into a car. The answer is easy. "Dorks," one woman told me. "Every time I look over to see who is driving one of those cars, it's almost always a dork." That sure made me feel a lot better about the guy in the Reliant.

So remember guys—as far as women go, cars do not make the man. And while we're at it, neither do clothes. Because eventually you have to get out of the former and take off the latter.

Then you'll get down to what she *really* loves you for.

Postpartum Male Persons

The docs now say that *men* can suffer from postpartum blues. These are the same men whose bodies have experienced no hormonal lurches over the past nine months, who do not have an extra twenty-five pounds to stuff into their prematernity jeans, and who, as a rule, have not had to give up their jobs to stay home with a squalling, drooling bundle of joy who thoroughly terrifies them.

But suffer they do. Male postpartum blues is a very real, but very unexplored phenomenon, according to some docs who Study These Things. In fact their study revealed that 62 percent of new fathers suffered postpartum blues. Which is certainly very modern and sensitive of these guys.

According to the docs, here are some of the travails these poor darlings endure:

1. Loss of Sleep. This is because sometimes a new father tries to help by taking upon himself the burden of one late-night feeding. This of course makes him very exhausted the next morning when he gets up. Unlike the new mother, for whom there is no morning because she is always up.

2. Loss of Efficiency. This exhaustion can lead to decreased job productivity. Women do not suffer from this because they know it's perfectly simple to care for a baby so long as you don't plan to do anything else in life. Including brushing your teeth.

3. Loss of Health. This exhaustion also reduces a new father's resistance to colds. Especially since no one is preparing proper meals for him.

4. Inability to Concentrate. One man reports that he finds himself picking up the remote control, pointing it at the kid, and pressing the mute button. Apparently it is difficult to write the great American novel when a baby is crying all the time.

5. Sense of Isolation. Many men rely on the little woman for emotional support. With the birth of their baby, they no longer get all the attention they so surely deserve.

6. Disruption of Sex Life. Try as he might to rise above these things, it isn't easy for a new father. Unlike his wife, who is forced to accept that she isn't capable of breastfeeding a baby, even though trillions of toothless *National Geographic* ladies have been doing this for years, men have trouble dealing gracefully with these little blows to their sexual egos.

7. Loss of Income. Now we're getting down to it. One more mouth to feed is bad enough. But having one less paycheck to do it with, well that can be terribly depressing.

8. Sudden Tearfulness. See Items 6 and 7.

So there you have it. Straight from the wonderful world of stress 'n' science. I suppose new dads have a right to sing the blues, postpartum or otherwise.

I just think they might abruptly shorten their lifespans if they sing them anywhere where the new moms can hear them.

GIRL
NOTES

Someday My Prince Will Still Come . . .

Dear Gloria Steinem:

I don't know how *you* felt when Walt Disney's *Cinderella* was just rereleased again, but I thought you should know how this 1950 movie sat with some 1980s female urchins. After all, these are the urchins you and I and Bella and Betty and Letty and Marlo have free-to-be-you-and-me'd, the ones we have worked on ever so diligently to shape up female horizon-wise.

And as all of us liberated ladies know, when we look back on our misspent youth in the fifties, there was nary a movie more insidious, more crippling, more mutant than Uncle Walt's *Cinderella*—with its blatant helplessness, low self-image, and someday-my-prince-will-come mindset.

Of course NOW membership aside, some of us still have to admit the film did have a certain magic and was probably the most memorable ninety minutes we've ever had in a movie theater.

Which must have been the reason I was drawn back to see it this weekend. Accompanied by the aforementioned female urchins —Alexis and Sara, both age eight. Just about my age when I first saw *Cinderella*.

But then these were eighties eight-year-olds. Girls who popped candy into their mouths from boxes inscribed SAY NO TO DRUGS. Girls who discussed at length the merits of their favorite Chicago

Black Hawks players. Girls who also discussed the possibility of growing up to be cops. Girls who asked not if I was married, but if I was *still* married. And if I wasn't, did I think my children would live in my house or their dad's? These were girls who were extremely well versed in the spectrum of vagaries out there. These were not girlie girls. These were girls who know the deal.

And they were girls who, even though they've never seen the Disney film, were certainly well apprised of the Cinderella story. They were girls who discussed the concept of princes while we were waiting for the movie to begin, and agreed with immense second-grade savvy that "guys like that are pretty hard to find."

And then the movie began. With that wonderfully saccharine song, "A Dream Is a Wish Your Heart Makes" the shimmery castle in the distance, all those chirpy little birds and adorable-ized little mice whipping up a ball gown for Cinderella, the well-timed arrival of the Fairy Godmother, the glory of pumpkins turning into coaches, the splendor of silvery glass slippers, and, above all, the heart-stopping moment when the prince spots our gal, Cindy, and sweeps her off her feet into True Love Land.

So, Gloria, we sat there. Me and the eighties female urchins. The ones who know about dee-vorce and child abuse and drugs and Dr. Ruth. And I asked them what they thought about this movie. I don't know how to tell you this, but, Gloria, they *loved* it. I of course asked them why.

And Alexis told me. "Because it was just so real."

Sorry, Glor.

Ooooh . . . What Shoulders

Another underwear breakthrough from Frederick's of Hollywood. The World's First Padded Shoulder Bra. For those of you who have been on Krypton for the past four years or so, there has been an alarming trend in The Fashion World toward gargantuan shoulders on normal-size women. No matter that this is a completely ridiculous look unless you are standing in a smoke-filled room singing something torchy with the Benny Goodman band behind you. The Fashion World has spoken to the American woman.

The interesting thing, however, is that The Fashion World has NOT spoken to the American man. At least not about shoulder pads on women. I, however, have. And these are some of the responses from some very "today" kind of guys:

• "I feel that if shoulder pads help a woman defend herself against a pass rush, then they are a real good idea."

• "On a tall woman from far away they can make her seem more attractive. But you put your arm around her, and feel that first killer squish, you realize how truly repulsive they are."

• "They are loathsome. Without question the worst fashion trend to come along since culottes—an invention that managed to make even Angie Dickinson look like she had fat knees and stubby little legs."

• "On short girls with no neck, it really promotes the old fire hydrant profile."

• "It seems to me that they are yet another deception further underlining the old adage: What you see is *not* what you get."

Thus, it is no surprise that Frederick's, the folks that built an empire on deceptive protuberances, should bring us The World's First Padded Shoulder Bra. After all, they brought America it's first padded bra in 1949, and then the first padded girdle (surely the all-time contradiction in terms) in 1951.

You are wondering, I suppose, just how I happen to have such salient undergarment statistics right at my journalistic fingertips. Well, as it happens, I have just returned from the world's first, and only . . . Bra Museum. It is located at Frederick's of Hollywood. In Hollywood. Where else. I wouldn't exactly say it's right up there with the Louvre and Uffizi, but in its own quirky way, it's a definite Must-See. Especially the fifties' styles they have labeled "Missiles and Snow Cones." But I digress . . .

So here we stand at what surely must be one of The Great Moments in Underwear History. But what do we make of the World's First Padded Shoulder Bra? Is this just one more Women's Lib-male copycat motif—like briefcases and ties and dull gray suits? Or is it one giant step in the other direction? Is it counter-liberation?

I mean why go to all that trouble to finally ditch the falsies if we are going to bring them back and put them three inches to the north?

Oink, Oink

How would you vote on the following question:

It is better to be a man □
It is better to be a woman □
(Vote only once.)

Up until now, I suspect the votes would have been pretty evenly split. But a recent piece of wondrous info makes it incredibly obvious that it is definitely better to be a female.

Here is the reason . . . only females get pregnant. And if you are a pregnant female, it is now possible, nay, it is even recommended, that you gain THIRTY-FIVE POUNDS during your pregnancy!

THIRTY-FIVE POUNDS! Do you believe that? The Public Health Service says if a mother gains thirty-five pounds, she diminishes the chances of delivering a low birth-weight baby and risking a fetal death. Thirty-five *guilt-free* pounds! Five hundred and sixty *guilt-free* ounces! Fifteen point nine *guilt-free* kilos! Any way you cut it, there is nothing quite as delicious, as poetic, and as unfathomably decadent as being granted THIRTY-FIVE POUNDS' worth of *fully sanctioned* pigging out.

Up until now, it had usually been recommended that expectant moms put on NO MORE THAN TWENTY POUNDS. Now, I know even twenty pounds sounds like a lot. Until you are the person who is actually pregnant. Because a pregnant person is chronically ravenous. Once she has finished being chronically nauseous.

In fact, this transformation happens overnight. One day she can't look a saltine in the eye. And the next day she wants blueberry pancakes, eggs over easy, and a double order of sausages. And only because of the twenty-pound limit does she hold off on the hash browns.

Let me explain to you how wonderful it feels to engage in licensed gluttony. I have been pregnant twice. And there are indeed many annoying things about being in that peculiar state. For instance, when you are pregnant, each time you look down at your legs you notice they are sporting a new network of blue veins. And when you are pregnant you must always be approximately a stone's throw from the nearest powder room. And when you are pregnant you have to pretend that some stupid breathing exercises are going to erase all the searing, violent pain of actually delivering a baby.

However, all of that pales in light of two shimmering, splendiferous facts. Fact #1: When you are pregnant, you no longer have to suck in your stomach. Fact #2: When you are pregnant, if you want to have pasta with a side order of french fries, you can actually do it. Up to a point. (The point formerly having been twenty pounds.)

But *this*. This is more than we dared hope for. This is almost twice as many pounds as they gave us before. No matter that the weight has to be taken off afterward. We spend the rest of our lives dieting anyway. But who cares? Not when you can wallow in luxuriant, remorse-free, medically approved gorging.

This is something no man, unless he is Robert De Niro porking up for a part in a movie, is ever going to have an opportunity to indulge in. This is uncensored face-stuffing, unbridled belly-building, and unhampered culinary indulgence.

This is the greatest. It's enough to make a forty-four-year-old woman consider the possibility of yet another baby.

I didn't say that—did I?

Bring Back Those Brush Rollers, Mama

The fundamental reason for this country's shockingly high teen-age pregnancy rate can be traced directly to the blow dryer.

I refer to nothing kinky. But four out of every ten American girls age fourteen to twenty become pregnant. I am convinced this shocking statistic would never have existed if it were not for the invention of this insidious little appliance. An appliance that has probably done more to undermine the moral values of this country than even R-rated movies or rock and roll music.

The main reason is this. Before blow dryers came on the scene, the young girls of America had no free time during which they could get into trouble. In the old days, a sweet young thing couldn't go gallivanting around at night. She was home. Because she had to set her hair. She had to gunk each section with styling goop, set it in tiny rows of eight trillion clips, and wait, yes, WAIT for it to dry. There were no portable hair dryers for the masses in the mid-fifties. Hairdos were an all-night ordeal requiring pounds of unattractive hardware, the wearing of which made one virtually unpresentable from 8:30 P.M. to approximately the same hour the following morning.

Additionally, the dos of yesteryear were very precisely regimented little affairs. None of this loosey-goosey, swingy look that can be blown dry in ten minutes and then the girl is out the door and into Lordknowswhat. Dips had to fall just so, spit curls had to be scrupulously anchored at the right angle, and most menacing and capricious of all, the ridge in one's page-boy fluff had to look as if it were drawn around the head with a compass, or the whole effort was for naught.

Besides being time consuming and exacting, Life Before Blow-Dry involved a nice healthy dose of suffering. There is indeed no suffering quite like the suffering of trying to sleep on about two dozen brush rollers. Blow-drying teaches nothing about suffering. Or about consequences. But you show me a girl whose head is covered by metal mesh and plastic bristles, and I'll show you a girl keenly aware of bodily pain and of consequences. Girls aware of bodily pain and consequences are not girls who are likely to become pregnant girls.

But enough philosophizing. Let us take a look at the statistics. It was in the early seventies that hand-held blow dryers first began to take hold. And between 1970 and 1979 surveys report that pre-marital sexual activity went up by two thirds! I suppose you think it's sheer coincidence. Don't make me laugh.

I know it will be a few years until the world starts accepting my theory. And until then, I am prepared to be the object of ridicule. But mark my words. When it comes to halting the soaring teenage pregnancy rate, it's not going to be sex education or contraception or any of that stuff, which drives the Moral Majority up the wall. There's just one thing we have to do.

Toss out those 1,200-watt superstylers and bring back the page-boy fluff with the precision ridge. Then you'll see a nation of young women we can be proud of again.

The Anguish of Accessorizing

It has to do with the right scarves and the right shoes and the right jewelry, and the women's magazines call it "accessorizing."

Accessorizing is ostensibly the thing that makes a *good* look into a *great* look. I personally don't know much about either of those looks since I am real grateful to just pull off a *presentable* look. I've never accessorized anything in my life.

If I buy a blue dress, I walk out of the store with a blue dress. Unless the saleslady tells me it *needs* something. If it *needs* something I tell her to *find* me something. Or else I don't walk out of the store with the blue dress. Because I know I will never find the thing it needs. Because the dress doesn't need just something. It needs Just the Right Thing. And it's very hard to find Just the Right Thing. People who find Just the Right Thing are people who LOVE to shop. Or people who are French.

But not me. I feel fully dressed if I have on one black knit dress with a florentine gold chain. And I hardly think the chain counts as an accessory since I have been wearing it for sixteen years and only take it off on days when I am giving birth. So I am the last person in the world you would expect to go overboard accessorizing a dress.

But I just bought this dress. It cost $135. This is pretty expensive for me but I am going to wear it on the "Today" show and sit next to Jane Pauley who puts on $800 dresses at four in the morning, so I figure $135 isn't that terrible.

Terrible is what the belt I fell in love with cost. It cost $115. In my wildest, most extravagant, most decadent daydreams I never planned to be the owner of a three-figure belt. Imelda can own a three-figure belt, Jackie can own a three-figure belt, but it is morally reprehensible for suburban housewives with serious car pool commitments to own a three-figure belt.

I bought the belt.

It makes the dress really wonderful. Even I can see that. I tell myself that people from Seattle to Boston will always remember me as an author who knew how to accessorize. I tell myself not to think of it as a $135 dress with a $115 belt, but rather as a $250 outfit—which will still be a K mart special in the shadow of Jane Pauley's morning ensemble.

And finally I tell myself that what I have just done means that I am obviously insane. And that soon they will be coming for me with a straitjacket.

Which, thank God, at least comes nicely accessorized . . .

Regarding Gray Hair and Purple Leather Jeans

Go figure it.

Approximately three years ago when Mom's hair started to gray a teensy, tiny bit, the child, who was then the charming age of thirteen, said, "Mom, I don't like it that you're getting older. Aren't you going to color your hair?"

The mom experienced several emotions. One was astonishment. One was tenderness. And one was a bit of confusion. She was astonished that her few gray hairs were even that noticeable. Especially to someone so preoccupied with rock and roll, and being cool, and junior high machinations. And she was very touched that this same person was truly concerned. And she was even more confused because she wasn't really sure what she wanted to do.

On one hand there was her fundamental vanity. A vanity no more excessive than the average neurotic woman who commits the heinous crime of actually growing older in a society that reveres all things taut and young. And on the other hand she felt adamantly that there was nothing more pathetic than a sixty-five-year-old woman running around in frosted hair, Reeboks, a jumpsuit, and dangle earrings, in some desperate imitation of someone decades her junior. Mom always said that one of the things she never intended to be was a geriatric vamp.

Of course Mom said this when she was on the green side of thirty-five. Which was a fairly safe place in which to make a smug little statement like that. Because, for the most part, gray hair and gravity still seemed like things that couldn't possibly happen to you for about a trillion years.

Funny thing about a trillion years. They arrive about in about two. Which meant that even though Mom still agreed philosophically with the premise that one accepts aging gracefully, when she looked in the mirror and saw the gray hair, graceful and accepting was not what she felt. Ultimately (as in a week after her daughter brought it up), she began coloring her hair. But a good part of the rationale was that she did it because her daughter wanted her to.

Funny thing about what daughter's want. It changes. By the time daughters are sixteen, they seem to want their moms to look perhaps a little more Mom-like. They figure, as they look in the mirror, that one good-looking woman is about all a household can handle, and quite clearly, they have decided to be it. Perhaps a mom with gray hair isn't such a bad idea after all.

This change comes simultaneously with the mom's increasing awareness that indeed her days of "cute" are numbered, but that need not mean she abandon herself to gray hair and terminally tasteful, discreet clothing. Thus it is no surprise that one day she makes an extremely wild and out-of-character purchase. She comes home with the finest pair of *purple leather jeans* you have ever seen.

Her daughter is of course appalled. As is everyone in the entire family. Purple leather jeans on a mom? Mom says why not? Mom says Jane Fonda wears them. Fine for Jane Fonda they say . . . but not for *you.*

The abhorrence and disgust engulfing that *"you"* is what finally convinces Mom. She takes the purple leather jeans back to the store.

And trades them in for a pair of *red* ones.

Hairdresser Divorce

There are divorces and there are divorces. But the most anguishing and traumatic divorce is one that doesn't involve lawyers, doesn't involve visitation rights, and doesn't involve property settlements.

The most traumatizing divorce in the world is when you divorce your hairdresser. When you decide that the time has come for a parting of the ways between you and Mr. René, you feel all the same emotions as if you were leaving a spouse: anxiety, resentment, guilt . . . Only when you divorce your hairdresser you feel one more thing. You feel real embarrassed.

That's because, unlike the marital kind of divorce, when you divorce your hairdresser, you almost never confront him. At least with your spouse, grievances are aired. But who has the nerve to tell Mr. René that the last cut he gave you left you looking like a woman born to wear sensible shoes and run potluck suppers in church basements. Unlike marital divorce, you don't want to hurt Mr. René's feelings. So you say not a word. You just never go back. Eight years under the trusty auspices of Mr. René, eight years of delicious gossip and shared confidences, and one day you just walk out the door never to be heard from again.

Even more embarrassing is the same-shop divorce. This just happened to Edna. Edna has been going to Delores for ten years. Last month Delores was on vacation when Edna needed an emergency haircut. So the receptionist offered Edna an appointment with Dino. Dino works the chair right next to Delores. Of course you know what happened. Edna got the best haircut of her life in the chair right next to Delores's.

So what's Edna to do? 1) She can sneak in to see Dino on Delores's day off. 2) She can confront Delores and tell her from now on she's going to Dino. 3) She can abandon the shop entirely. Or 4) She can adopt the Abraham solution. That's the one where Edna forces her daughter to come to this shop and sacrifices her to Delores while she starts going to Dino.

Edna has not been sleeping well lately.

Because she knows what you know. And you know that no matter what happens, you are doomed. Because someday you will step onto an elevator, and find yourself looking directly into the eyes of . . . your ex-hairdresser. This will happen on the morning before an afternoon appointment to get your roots done. Your hair will be two-toned, unwashed, and matted.

It's beauty parlor destiny.

Bringing Back
Ba-zooms

Talk about overreaction. Bras are back. Not only are bras back but boned bras are back. Not only are boned bras back, but boned bras worn bare are back.

It's true. I read it in the newspaper. The *dernier mot* from fashion-land is a long-line, multihooked, underwired undergarment. Only now it's not *under* the garment, it *is* the garment. After thirteen months of being told it's chic to wear designer undershirts under our blouses, we're being told not only is it okay to abandon the undershirts, but that it's also okay to abandon the blouses. The look we are being shown is a basic black tailored suit open to the waist over a bordello red corset—something of a cross between E.F. Hutton and Cyndi Lauper— And last week European designers Jean-Paul Gaultier and Ungaro were showing something called bra-topped dresses in their spring collections. Zounds.

I for one am thrilled about the demise of undershirts. It is very hard to support a look that offers one so little support. Undershirts do not do wonders for the self-image of any post thirty-two-year-old female who has borne a child or two and may find herself in the odiously inescapable position of succumbing to gravity.

However, corsets don't do a whole lot for a girl's self-image, either. Not if she takes her liberation semi-seriously. These harnesses evoke a real retro look. Pour your parts in, take a deep breath, truss up all the fastenings, and *shazam!* You've got the waist of Scarlett O'Hara, the pulchritude of Lillian Russell, and (after wearing it longer than thirty minutes), the disposition of Joan Crawford. Why on earth would we want to take a giant step backward and step into a contraption like this?

This is an illusion machine. A "bustier" (todays chi-chi nomer for what we called "merry widows" in the fifties) is the very stuff anatomical misconceptions were made of. It has taken years to dismantle the notion that breasts were not two uniformly conical protuberances firmly anchored no lower than three inches below our shoulders. Years.

Other than faces, breasts are probably the most obvious and variable aspect of our anatomy. And by finally acknowledging that variability, we got rid of all the pads and pointy cups and painful pushup hardware we'd all forced ourselves into for so long. And we were left with Just Breasts. And for most of us that meant not a lot of voluptuousness, not a lot of volume, but still a lot of vulnerability.

Most of us feel very unresolved about our breasts. It's not just a matter of not being big enough or small enough or shaped this way or that. But we never really have quite figured out what to do with them when they're not in use. They are sort of hard to ignore. And unlike everything else that's quintessentially a private part of our bodies, there's always been something quasi-public about them. We're always making a statement with them.

For the last few years our statement has been one of freedom, independence, individuality, and nonconstraint. In the sixties we were rather defiant about it, but as it became apparent that bralessness was not the best look or the most comfortable situation for all of us, we returned to some form of bracketing, though considerably more pliant and humane than yesteryear's. We had almost gotten to the point where our breasts were integrated into our lives. And now comes this.

The recontainerizing of our mammary glands. Don't tell me some clowns in Paris are going to convince us to resubmit our breasts to a device that has them all cantilevered, semi-spilling out, and thrust up and forward like some fleshy horizontal shelf.

Why would we want to put back the armor when we've almost won the war?

Nail Stress

Darling, I know this is painful to talk about. But it's time someone came out of the closet. And I just think all you ladies who are victims of, of, of . . . okay, I'll say it . . . Nail Stress should hear this.

You know what Nail Stress is. It's that complete, total, and utter panic you go through every time one of your nails—OHMYGOD!—breaks. It's what sends you dashing to your neighborhood nail emporium for surgery. Because unless you can get a transplant, a patch, or an emergency sculpt, well, darling, face it, your whole life risks being shattered.

I'm not talking to you ladies who go to your local beauty salon and let Madge slap a coat or two of Revlon on while your tresses are being crimped. I'm talking about those of you who are passionate about perfect nails. Who have been through the rigors of acrylic ovals. We have known the rapture of the silk wrap. Who perceive that two-hour appointment at your friendly nail boutique as the religious high point of your week. Women like Lorraine, who, looking down at her freshly glossed talons, told me without batting an eyelash, "If I had to list my top ten priorities, I'd say my nails are only number three. My husband and my children come first."

I think we have to get this thing under control. And one good way to undo this obsession might be to hear what some American men have to say about women with long, lacquered fingernails:

• "I see them and it makes me wonder, what does this woman do in life that she doesn't need her fingers?"

• "It's confusing. On one hand they say, 'Look at me, I'm sexy,' but on the other they also say, 'I am a woman who definitely does *not* like to be mussed.' And most men like their women real muss-able."

• "It's easy. I see vanity. I see bitchiness. I see a real prima donna."

Now I was all set to argue with those gentlemen, to explain to them that women suffering from Nail Stress *can* be women of principle, of substance, of sensitivity. But then I went to one of our more shimmering nail emporiums and overheard the following remarks . . .

• "I love coming here in the morning and then just hanging around the salad bar afterwards. You don't feel so guilty going out for lunch when you're doing something constructive—like getting your nails done."

• "The worst moment in my life was the night I put in the meatloaf and then discovered that my acrylic nail had come off. Of course, I had no one to blame but myself. I shouldn't have been cooking in the first place."

Tsk tsk. Ladies. You should be ashamed. Even the proprietor of the salon thinks things have gotten out of hand. "We're busy from five-thirty in the morning to nine at night. It's crazy. Nails have become a terrible priority."

How terrible?

"Well let me put it this way. Last month a woman got a call from Florida. Her mother had just had a stroke and was dying. But she came here first on her way to the airport."

That's how terrible.

Sports Illustrated Strikes Again

Ladies, this is not going to be one of your better weeks.

A woman in New York named Jule Campbell has seen to that. Just like she has for the past twenty-two years. Jule Campbell is the editor of the annual *Sports Illustrated* swimsuit issue, which will hit the stands on Wednesday. Thus we are exactly ninety-six hours away from the day that constitutes the annual low point for the self-esteem of the American woman.

I asked Jule Campbell if every year when she picks these swimsuit models, she purposely picks the ones who would make us women feel the rottenest. She laughed her powerful magazine-editor laugh and said, "Of course not." But rotten is exactly how we feel. We don't even have to be fat to feel rotten. We just have to be normal. Normally imperfect. A dimple here, a vein there, nothing major, just a few routine shortcomings.

Which, when compared to the bronzed, airbrushed, glossed, and depilatoried specimens of taut, transcendant perfection in *Sports Illustrated,* make us feel like Quasimodo's twin sister. There are two reasons for this. One is that women are slightly neurotic about these things. The other is that they have reason to be—men are not very forgiving about the discrepancy between the way we look in a black maillot and the way Paulina Porizkova does.

Even men of substance, who love us for our brains and our sense of humor, who have long ago accepted the fact that there are Magazine Women and Real Life Women and never the twain shall meet, even these men are guilty. Take Donald, a man perfectly thrilled that his wife made the *Law Review* at the University of Chicago. "I have no problem accepting that Leslie doesn't look like a Playmate. It's easy. Playmates are fantasies. But there's something about *Sports Illustrated* that's different, maybe more real or credible. And I can't help sort of superimposing Leslie's head on those bodies and wondering . . ." Have a nice day, Leslie.

Anybody with a modicum of compassion knows that putting out a swimsuit issue in the dead of winter, when we women have lips that are chronically chapped, thighs that are chronically pale, and noses that are chronically runny, is a fairly hostile concept. We don't even have a fighting chance. And *Sports Illustrated* isn't the only offender. The swimsuit issues of both *Life* and *Inside Sports* have been out a couple of weeks. But neither delivers the large circulation (or emotional devastation) of *Sports Illustrated*'s swimsuit issue—an issue that sells 3.3 million copies, half a million more than the magazine's normal run.

So here we go again. The way we do every year. Just listen to how this issue makes us feel:

• "It's definitely *the* devastating post-holiday blow. Every year I despair, I groan, I go on a diet, and then I give up. I could chain myself to Nautilus machines for the rest of my life and still never look like that."

• "It's not fair. Two years ago I was all bundled up digging myself out of a snowbank on my way to exercise class. The mailman came up and delivered our *Sports Illustrated*. I took one look at that and just figured, 'What's the point?' "

• "Let me just say this. Plain and simple. It annoys the shit out of me."

However, ladies, there is one small ray of sunshine in all this. Right now, sitting inside an apartment, is a woman feeding a baby. Her belly is a bit crepe-y and she is riddled with postpartum stretch marks. And in four more days, when her husband's *Sports Illustrated* comes in the mail, she will know, for the very first time, the anguish that American women have been dealing with for years.

Her name is Christie Brinkley.

Heh. Heh. Heh.

HOLIDAY BLISSES, MISSES, AND GET-ME-OUTTA-THIS-ES

Dissolved Resolve

What is great about January 2 is that New Year's Eve is definitely gone.

What is not great about January 2 is that so is most of your willpower.

Here we are, exactly a day and half into the new year, and most of us are already sitting amidst a sea of shattered resolutions. I personally have just finished devouring one pound of stale Christmas cookies, have yelled at a child with such ferocity that he is currently looking up adoption agencies in the Yellow Pages, and have told a full-fledged lie to a neighbor who wanted to know if we had a wonderful time at her New Year's Eve party.

Also, without even thinking about it, I just brewed up real coffee with real molecules of cancer-causing caffeine in it, and only a half hour ago I stubbed my toe and said the s-word. Thus, in the first thirty-six hours of this brand new year I have already broken five of my top ten resolutions.

I could console myself with the thought that at least 50 percent of my resolutions are still in perfect condition. But that's about as consoling as telling yourself you are still a 50-percent virgin. In fact virginity is a lot like New Year's resolutions—it's definitely futile (and definitely no fun) to try and keep either of them. And with each, once you slip even a little bit, it's only a matter of time until you totally cave in.

However, January 2 is a day when most of us feel a lot worse about the collapsed state of our New Year's resolve than the collapsed state of our virginity. Therefore, let us consider why New Year's resolutions never work out.

First of all, New Year's comes at the wrong time of the year. There is no way that anyone can turn over a new leaf when there are no leaves left on the trees or the ground to turn over. I think New Year's should be on the first day of school. The day after Labor Day. That's the day when, even though we may have been out of school for decades, we feel like we are starting over. Like we have a clean slate. Like it's time to buy new clothes. Sign up for new therapy groups. Change the message on our answering machine. That's the time of year we are committed to change. And that's the time of year we are filled with optimism.

January is not a time in which most of us are capable of optimism. How can you be optimistic when all the grass is smothered by gritty snow? When it is dark by four thirty-five every afternoon? When the tomatoes taste like postcards? No, the logical time to harness resolve is the night before school starts.

The second reason New Year's resolutions never work out is that we make too many and we set up goals that are too hard to achieve. The whole trick is make a few resolutions and make them manageable. A person with a violent temper and bad manners shouldn't be expected to go through the year without saying the s-word. Therefore I'm revising my list of resolutions right now.

I'm not going to smoke. This should be pretty easy to manage since I've never smoked and I doubt I will start this year.

I'm not going to leave the air conditioner on when I go to work. This should be pretty easy to manage. For six months at least.

I'm not going to have an affair with Robert Redford. I'm almost positive I can stick to this.

Unless he asks.

Homegrown
Valentines

Before you spend your entire lunch hour today picking through the picked-over racks of valentines, let me ask you this: Are you giving a valentine that will be cherished and saved and wrapped in pink ribbons?

I don't mean it has to be big, or satiny, or fancy. But imagine how much it would mean if it was actually a valentine penned by you. America has become addicted to greeting-card giving and long-distance phoning, which means that actual pen-on-paper personal love missives seem to have become a thing of the past. And it makes me wonder what on earth we'll put in pink ribboned packets and browse through during our twilight years. I doubt most of us are saving our Hallmarks.

Why should we? All they represent is someone else's version of the sender's ostensible feelings. Given the fact that the average American sends twenty-five greeting cards a year (not including Christmas), it would seem not many of us are willing to tough it out with pen and paper anymore. We're embarrassed, we're unimaginative, we've got nothing to say. Oh come on. What makes something homemade so cherishable isn't the card itself, it's that someone you love anguished over its creation.

When I was growing up, our family was a relentless producer of homemade greetings. We were firm believers that toil was a permissible substitute for talent. However, sometimes the two miraculously merged, as in my nine-year-old brother's poetic anniversary commemoration of my parent's wedding:

> *Mom's hair was brown and messy*
> *Dad's hair was growing less-y*
> *They looked so cute, the two of them,*
> *Oh yessy.*

We weren't just limited to poetry. We did everything from takeoffs on the Gettysburg Address to song parodies of vintage hits like "How Much Is That Doggie in the Window?" Year after year, our handwriting growing less primitive, our themes growing more threadbare, we barraged each other with words that were wondrously corny. Wondrously clever.

Even my father penned incredible stuff to my mom. During an apparently rocky year he gave this one to her:

> *We're out of a job and we don't have much dough,*
> *Our ship of life is in a bad blow.*
> *We're going to make port soon and find calmer seas,*
> *We'll get a strong steady wind and a tropical breeze.*
> *Your gentleness and tenderness play the major part,*
> *Because you are my life, my soul, and my heart.*

This from a man who was ashamed of his spelling and loathe to be anything less than regulation macho. But gradually Daddy and the rest of us abandoned our artistic efforts and capitulated to the convenience of mass-produced sentiments—very expedient, but not the sort of thing you collect in pink ribbons and savor decades later.

So this year I told my guy what I wanted from him. It won't take a lot of talent, just a little bit of time, a modicum of creative effort, and an enforced moment of reflection. And I don't care if he hands me a piece of legal paper that says,

> *Roses are red,*
> *Violets are blue.*
> *This is a valentine*
> *From me to you.*

Because I'll love it. And I've got my pink ribbon all ready.

My Mother/NOT Myself

It was great entertainment, but if *Terms of Endearment* made the definitive statement on mothers and daughters, we are in major trouble. Most daughters would prefer not to become terminally ill in order to resolve the exasperating struggles they are still lurching through with their moms.

The struggle revolves around approval. Even though we profess to be beyond this, at some gut level, many of us still nurture this intense yearning for unconditional acceptance. This is rather odd considering the great lengths many daughters go to in order to become something approximately 180 degrees removed from what their mothers were.

I'm not just talking about Working Moms today versus At Home Moms yesterday—that's part of it—but also the whole stylistic thing. Most of us don't do life the way our moms did. If she was an organizational wizard, we tend to be chaotic; if she was real social, we tend to be a bit isolationist; if she went in for face-lifts, we don't even wear makeup.

In fact, the very heart of the mother-daughter dynamic is this chronic tug-of-war. Daughters are hell-bent on disengagement and mothers instinctively strive for fusion. It's built into the species. That ridiculous fashion of mother-daughter dresses may have bitten the dust a few decades ago, but mothers still can't help wanting to mold daughters in their own image. I find myself doing that with my own daughter. This year we took a jazz dancing class together on Saturday mornings. It was one of my peak motherhood experiences—I was absolutely thrilled that, like me, she is passionate about dance. Suppose she had been passionate about the accordian? I hate the accordian. Would I have been as approving and supportive of that? I would have tried, but it would have been a something of a charade.

And daughters always know when it's a charade. My friend Suzanne knows that even though her mother says she understands why Suzanne divorced her husband, she basically disapproves of Suzanne's divorcing when she stuck it out all these years with her own less-than-Mr.-Wonderful. Suzanne's divorce seems like something of a repudiation of the choice she made with her life.

Same with my friend Linda. Linda is a real capable, high-energy woman who keeps a full-time job and family afloat without a lot of nail-biting or hair-tearing. Linda's mom, a much more tentative woman, who found family raising fairly nerve-racking, always tells Linda, "I think it's *just great* that you can go off to a business meeting at night and tell the kids to grab some cheeze for dinner." But Linda knows that Mom doesn't really think it's great. It makes Mom a little ticked off that she spent twenty years deliberating over string beans or brussel sprouts with dinner tonight, and Linda just breezes through life with a briefcase, a housekeeper, and six flavors of yogurt. She thinks Linda's kids will probably be screwed up. They will be. But Linda figures she was screwed up, too, and at least she's screwing up her kids her way and not her mother's.

And since she's gone so far out of her way to do things so differently from Mom, she's also beginning to realize how unfair it is to expect unconditional acceptance from Mom. Moms are people too. They come with limitations. And just because they have them doesn't mean they've failed us, no matter how much we prefer to think so during our years at the shrink.

I'm just beginning to figure that out. And I was thinking I'd give my mom a great present for Mothers Day. I was going to, *ta dum*, forgive my Mom. But even I realized how incredibly pretentious that was—there was really nothing to forgive. The only thing to do was to *accept*. Accept that unconditional acceptance from our mothers is a pretty unrealistic expectation. To really accept that and to let go of that need would be a terrific Mother's Day present. Terrific for her, and especially terrific for me.

You Remember Daddy, Don't You, Dear?

$\mathbf{Y}$ou don't have to be Margaret Mead to know that the results of the survey were pretty devastating. The question being asked was: What is the hardest thing about being a daddy? The survey respondents were a unique bunch: none of them came from divorced homes. All of them had full-time daddies on the premises. So to speak.

These twenty-two third graders ostensibly had the best of all possible worlds. Not only were they living in two-parent families, but these were families where daddies had jobs, mommies drove Volvos, and most homesteads came equipped with computers and color TVs. The fathers were judges, and TV executives and commodities brokers, and lawyers, or had jobs like "I don't know exactly what he does, but he's president of A&P or Super-Plus or whatever."

These were kids who could pile in the car every summer and go on family vacations, kids who looked like they have the closest version available in the eighties of the Norman Rockwell School of Family Life. Except when Norman Rockwell painted those pictures, Daddy was *in* the picture. These kids have daddies who don't seem to be much in the picture at all.

According to the survey, the hardest thing about being a dad is that Dad is not ever there to *be* the dad. Most of us grew up feeling our dads weren't around too much, either, but with all the talk about paternal participation in the past decade, things still haven't changed a whole lot. "He's always gone," was the concise observation of 80 percent of the two-parent kids. Partly it was business trips. It didn't matter to the kids if Dad had gone to Paris or Akron; no dad was no dad. Postcards and presents do not a daddy at the kitchen table make.

A daddy at the kitchen table is hardly guaranteed even if he happens to be in town. According to two thirds of the kids, Dad leaves for work well before breakfast and comes home from work well after dinner. A dad may get home by seven or eight, "but he's too wiped out to play ball." About five kids had dads who were home by six, which sounded pretty promising until two mentioned that "And after dinner he always starts working some more."

However it should be noted that not one survey respondent exhibited any petulance or placed any blame. Instead these kids were almost wearily acquiescent. They not only accepted that Daddy HAS to work (none felt Dad LIKED to work), but they actually felt sorry for the guy. They were even bizarrely empathetic. Take birthdays. Nothing hurts worse than having Dad out of town on your birthday. But instead of describing that in terms of a nine-year-old's deprivation, one said, "It's sad cause your mom has to tell you all the things he really wanted to say to you himself," and another said, "Dads always feel bad on birthdays cause they don't really know you well enough from day to day to figure out what you really want for a present."

Don't really know you well enough from day to day . . . That's the statement that every divorced father fears most, and yet these nuclear family dads are hearing the same thing: The only time that Dad is around is on weekends. Again, without a modicum of recrimination. They all just shrug their shoulders and recite: Dad has to work/so we can have money/so we can buy *things*.

"Well if you had to choose between having Daddy at home every night for six months or having your five-speed bike, your videocassette recorder, and day camp this summer, what would you choose?" (Please kid, give the right answer.)

She doesn't. She gives the honest one. "I dunno."

Happy Father's Day. At least the kids understand why you're out there busting your backside. For *things*, Daddy, for *things*.

Haute Halloween

The worst part about Halloween is the Homemade Costume Imperative. I never even knew from homemade costumes until I moved into this neighborhood.

It's not that this neighborhood is full of women with a lot of free time on their hands. But it's full of working women who have taken on Halloween as the moment to prove they are ultracapable wondermoms. These women may be in meetings till six every night, and on business trips during their kid's first dramatic appearance as a carrot in Peter Rabbit, but I tell you, when it comes to Halloween, there is no way that any child of theirs is going to appear in anything reeking of Woolworth's.

When I was a kid (with a nonworking mother), it was perfectly permissible to don a sleazy cheesecloth costume that cost $1.29, had a durability guarantee of approximately 6.2 minutes, tied in the back like a dopey pair of jammies, and had a picture of Tinker Bell on it. If your cheesecloth jammies had a picture of Tinker Bell on it, you WERE Tinker Bell. If your cheesecloth jammies had a picture of Snow White on it, you WERE Snow White. Everyone wore cheesecloth jammies with a picture on it unless they had moms who went in for *creative* costumes.

There were two motifs for creative costumes in the fifties. One was the Lone Ranger creative motif, which consisted of a cowboy hat, a holster with two guns, and a tasteful white mask. Not too taxing to throw together. The other was the Mary Heartline motif (remember the world's oldest living drum majorette?), which consisted of one demi-baton and a pair of dazzling white boots—with tassels. And that was about it for creative costumes.

Well forget creative. What today's moms are going for in the Halloween costume department transcends creative. It's practically couture. These women sew and paste and collage themselves into a frenzy for weeks before the big event. Two years ago, I counted, and there were seventeen humongous cardboard Rubik's Cubes trick or treating at my door. With twistable parts. The year before there were twenty-one gargantuan, custom-made Pac-Mans at my door. All stitched and wired into offensively yellow voracious perfection. Every year there is a minimum of five or six three-foot Campbell's Soup cans. And last year, there were two papier mâché Apple Computer systems (we're talking printers, screens, and two disc drives) who came knocking in search of nourishment. Not a cowboy, not a ghost, not a dime-store Tinker Bell in the bunch. Every creature who came calling was a veritable masterpiece of pop art. Creativity run rampant.

This poses a real problem for those of us who tend to be a bit thin in the imagination and artistic talent department. You can't fathom the silent shame we feel when our pathetic efforts are held up to the general pièce de résistance caliber of the arts 'n' crafts contingency. There's just no way little Johnny is going to feel terrific if his mom threw sheet over him, cut out two eyes, and said, "Here, you're a ghost" when his best friend is making the rounds as the Sears Tower.

I say we call a halt to this escalation of couture costuming. Halloween is for kids, not for moms to make their own personal swellness statements. I say let's get back to basics. Think how much better we'll be all around. Your ego won't be on the line, and though your trick or treater's disguise might not wind up at the Museum of Contemporary Art, for $2.99 at least the kid will be in something flame retardant. I say . . . support your local Woolworth's.

The Real
Thanksgiving
Turkey

Of all the hallowed Thanksgiving traditions taking place today in the American home, there is none that has quite the emotional impact of this one—The First Return Visit of the First-Semester College Student. Because the first Thanksgiving home is the moment the student always chooses to show all of us he left behind HOW MUCH HE HAS CHANGED.

It is quite astounding, when you think about it, that, after spending eighteen years under your roof, in only ten short weeks under another roof this person has managed to do a total 180° on everything that until last September he professed to be, and to believe in.

It starts with his basic look. It's as if you put a prince on the airplane and when you go to fetch him ten weeks later, off comes a toad. (It seldom works in the other direction, at least not for this first return engagement.) If he left looking preppie, he comes back looking punk; if he left looking California, he comes back looking New England; if he left looking designer, he comes back looking generic. Ten little weeks in a dorm and the entire wardrobe you outfitted him with has already been rendered defunct.

As have many of the assumptions you thought were well imbued. Assumptions like: Even though you're no longer in school, it's possible you are an intelligent being too. A first-semester college student thinks he is very smart. About everything. For instance, in the entire eighteen years during which he lived with you, he never once posed any questions about the general cash-flow situation in the household from which he has always obtained food, shelter, and a weekly allowance.

Now, after a mere two months in Intro. to Economics, after having read all the way to page 127 of the Paul Samuelson text, he's got serious theories. He thinks you are a real cretin for not socking your savings into short-term CDs. He wants to know why you have never made any major investments in the stock market. (Somehow he hasn't quite grasped that coming up with a college tuition precludes making any major investments in the stock market. Maybe that's in Intro. to Economics II.)

A first-semester student also feels compelled to attack your basic political stance. No mind that up until two months ago, the only time he was ever passionate about politics was when his girlfriend ran for secretary-treasurer of the pep club. Now, he has just completed a term paper comparing and contrasting Plato's *Republic* with Rousseau's *The Social Contract.* This qualifies him to be the resident philosopher king in the family, and to point out to you that even though you thought you were left of center, you've never been anything but a closet fascist. (Words like "closet fascist" tend to abound during the Thanksgiving Visit of the First-Semester College Student.)

Additionally, you go to great lengths to cook all the kid's vegetarian favorites like tofu souffle and three-sprout casserole. He then tells you he's abandoned that dietary mode and returned to the wonderful world of chocolate and carbohydrates. Food to study by.

Finally, you decide to give him an early Christmas present—two tickets to the Springsteen concert on Saturday night. Coolly, he suggests that you return them. His music appreciation course has gotten him seriously into opera, so perhaps they can be exchanged for tickets to *Der Rosenkavalier.*

There is absolutely no point during the entire visit where the student does not make it a point to make a point about something. It is a grueling five days.

But Sunday night does come. The Student boards the plane. The First Return Visit is over. Few of them are ever as dramatic, bemusing, and insufferable as this. And you actually survived it. That's something definitely worth giving thanks over.

Christmas Memo
from Mom

Memo to Santa from Me:

You must be sick and tired of getting all this mail that says I WANT THIS for Christmas, and I WANT THAT for Christmas, so I figured I'd try a different approach. I figured I'd tell you exactly what I DON'T WANT for Christmas. My Christmas would be almost perfect if I do NOT receive any of the following items.

Item #1. The Annual early December phone call from my sister-in-law. This is the one where she calls up to tell me she is so bored because her Christmas shopping has been done for weeks. All her presents are purchased, wrapped, and mailed off. Especially the one to our mutual mother-in-law (guaranteeing that for the tenth straight year I will probably not be the recipient of the favorite daughter-in-law trophy). Then she tells me that all thirty-seven varieties of her Christmas cookies are baked, frosted, and tinned, and that she has just put the finishing touches on her famous gingerbread condo and resort complex. Dear Santa, I hate my sister-in-law in December.

Item #2. The Annual Requisition from Brutus Bunsbuster, Our Newspaper "Boy." Boy, my eye. There are no newspaper "boys" these days because they all have to be at least old enough to drive a car. None of them comes on foot anymore. Except on Christmas morning when they trudge forlornly through the snow up to our door, ring the doorbell, and say, "I hope I'm not disturbing you on this busy and joyful day, but I'm Brutus your faith-

ful and trusty news servant, and I just wanted to extend my
warmest greetings and good wishes to you and yours." Which is not
true, Santa. What Brutus really wants is five bucks. Actually, last
year Brutus changed the format. He sent a little printed card two
weeks in advance of Christmas that contained a sincere message of
peace and goodwill to all mankind. Then he included a stamped,
self-addressed envelope that had on the back "Be sure to enclose
your check, before sealing."

Item #3. The Annual Christmas Letter from Melodie and
Alphonse Sinkworth. Santa, I don't even know Melody and Alphonse Sinkworth. I think my husband went to grammar school
with one of them years ago. But those letters of theirs have tracked
us down for twenty-three years. Twenty-three years of saccharine,
detailed, appallingly mundane progress reports about four complete
strangers . . . "Dear Friends: As we celebrate our traditional
Christmas, with our mountain pine tree decorated with hand-
crafted ornaments, collected over the years, Alphie, Muffy, Wentworth, and I are thriving, happy, and much too *busy!!!* Our year has
been filled with the usual round of tennis, sailing, soccer (indoor
and out!!!), car pools, art classes, volunteering, studying, and fasci-
nating travels!!! We spent winter vacation in Vail (great!!!), spring
vacation in Disney World (marvelous!!!), summer vacation on Cape
Cod (super!!!). We've always loved to visit unspoiled, off-the-
beaten-path spots!!!

"As usual Buffy went to Camp Merrie-woode (where she
broke her left pinkie, but still managed to be fourth runner-up in
intermediate aquaplaning!!!). Wentworth's collection of "Roach
Clips from Many Lands" won All-District in the state science com-
petition. But he still had a bit of catching-up work to do before
beginning his freshman year at Farnsworth Remedial Military
Academy, so he didn't return to Camp Cutyourpartsoff this year. I
finally completed my est graduate work and I really feel the insights
I gained there helped enormously in my work as co-chairperson of
this year's Blossom Valley Recycled Cans Drive!!! And Alphie, well,
as usual, he just LOVES his job, and now that he's been promoted
to third vice president of the northeastern division, it's just work,

work, work!!! As we look to this great wonderful time of year, we all join in wishing you a special joyeaux Noel!!!

Santa, I know you can't stop her from writing, but if you could just jam the exclamation point key on her typewriter, it would really help a lot.

Keeping the Faith

Yes, Santa Claus, there is a Virginia.

And even though it is the 1980s and she lives half the time with her mommy and half the time with her daddy, and even though a girl she once knew now is pictured as a missing child on a milk carton, and even though the older brother of one of her friends is in a drug rehabilitation center, Virginia is still a kid. And she still needs to believe in you.

She's a lot different from the Virginia who wrote the New York *Sun,* back in 1897, pleading, "Please tell me the truth; is there a Santa Claus?" The paper's response, that classic editorial titled "Yes, Virginia, There Is a Santa Claus," was read over and over again to reassure generations of children that you really do exist.

Only now, Santa, I think it might be you who needs to be reassured. I bet you're wondering if there are any believers anymore. I'm sure there are days when you're sitting up there at the North Pole, putting some finishing touches on a wooden train, wondering why in the world you're bothering to sand and paint and glue, when the kid you are making it for is watching movies of the week on sexual abuse.

Kids are so savvy, so streetwise, so jaded these days, I worry that you might think they've lost their capacity for being bedazzled. I don't think they've lost it. They may have just lost touch with it. They've got a lot on their minds.

For instance, Virginia was recently told by her teacher that she was going to have to get a tutor in reading. Virginia burst into tears. Not because of the tutor. "But," she wailed, "it means I'm not going to be smart, and if I'm not going to be smart, how am I going to do in high school, and if I do bad in high school, how am I going to get into college, and if I don't go to college, how am I ever going to find a good job?" Virginia is nine, Santa, nine.

Nine is a time when historically the Virginias of the world may have lost the faith. So the interesting thing about today's Virginias is this: in spite of being prematurely neurotic about their MBA's, and in spite of having standing appointments with the school shrink, and in spite of knowing full well that the Benetton sweater they want is not manufactured at the North Pole (in fact that may be the only place left in the world where there is no Benetton), they have absolutely no intention of giving you up. They know they've already been robbed of great chunks of their childhood, and they're not about to relinquish what little is left. Especially if it's left in the wonderment sector.

That's why Virginia told her mother last week that she sure hoped some of the packages under the tree would still say, "From Santa Claus." She was real clear that without those gifts *from you*, it just wouldn't feel like Christmas. I thought you might want to know that. Because even though Virginia didn't write you this year, it doesn't mean she's stopped being a kid.

So don't give up on her, Santa. She hasn't given up on you. In fact, she asked me to ask you . . . which do you want this year—peanut butter or chocolate chip cookies?

Return to Spender

The worst part is that *this* isn't even the worst part.

The worst part is on December 26. When you have to return all this stuff.

Listen. Everyone knows that Christmas shopping is an ordeal. It frazzles the nerves, it depletes the pocketbook, it exhausts the imagination. But what makes it tolerable, in spite of all this, and in spite of the overheated stores and the overheated tempers, is that running through the entire odious procedure is a faint wisp of hope. Hope that all this searching and all this schlepping and all this scrambling will ultimately result in a gift or two that will Actually Please the designated recipient. Fools that we are.

Because every year when the last box has been opened, and the final tabulation comes in, the results are always the same. At least half the stuff is NO GO. And it becomes clear that you have exactly twenty-four hours before you're back in the stores again. This does not do great things for your Christmas cheer quotient.

It always starts with your basic remote control toy car. You had a minimum choice of thirty from which to choose. Even the cheapest of which was too expensive, because a cheap remote control car will be dead, inert, irreparably dysfunctional by 11:59 P.M. on December 25. The assumption is that a more expensive remote control car will last longer. But you know better than that. For another twenty bucks you might eek about one more week out of the old remote-control-car lifespan. But you've been through this before.

And ultimately you opted for the fast death. And you'll get what you paid for. Therefore it'll be back to Toys-Reverse-"R"-Us for sure.

Which won't be nearly as complicated a procedure as taking back all the teenage wearing apparel you've just finished buying. Now you have worked very hard this year to get the drift fashion-wise. You've studied the Esprit catalogue, you've lurked around the Guess? jeans departments, you've haunted The Limited. Nonetheless it is axiomatic that the child will be crestfallen when she opens everything. The pleats will be "too thin," or the buttons will be "too gross," or the pockets will be "too retarded." These are direct quotes from last year's rave reviews.

Of course the diciest holiday shopping quandry is What to Buy for Mom. Mom-buying is particularly problematic for two reasons. 1) Moms never live in the same town as you do, so it has to be from a store where *she* can return it. This limits you to K mart and Saks Fifth Avenue. The full spectrum. 2) Moms have everything. Except a VCR. Which they are afraid of. Thus, you wound up getting her what you always get her. A sweater—which she will tell you "is really lovely, but there is something about the sleeves . . ."

What all this means is simple. It takes you about forty shopping hours to buy enough things to disappoint everyone, and about forty returning hours to get it all back, and about forty bookkeeping hours to get all your records and receipts straight.

Which only goes to prove . . . it's less exhausting to earn the money than it is to spend it.

Extraterrestrial Trip Report

Day 1: Our landing on earth went very smoothly. Our spacecraft is well hidden in what appears to be a deserted forest. No one will ever see it. Unlike my last observation trip which occurred during the earthling time prism of summer, this visit the earthlings seem quite disinterested in the woods, the sea, and the outdoors. Instead, they cram themselves inside hot, noxiously musical, encapsulated corridors called malls.

The earthlings do not seem to be happy in these malls. And yet they return day after day. It is quite disconcerting to observe them as they race from vendor to vendor frantically laying in supplies for some sort of event that will be occurring in the next few weeks. There are signs everywhere saying FIFTEEN MORE SHOPPING DAYS. These signs seem to torment the earthlings. Apparently the deadline for this even looms ever closer. I will report more tomorrow.

Day 2: I am beginning to get the drift. The event is some sort of gargantuan ritual in honor of the goddess of commerce. I'm not quite sure of the precise reason that it takes place. But large-scale appeasement of the earthling children is definitely a big part of it. Evidently the big earthlings will go to any extreme in order to satisfy the material whims of the little earthlings. This is my conclusion after having spent fifteen solid hours (the sign said "open from 9 till midnite . . .") in a rather bizarre emporium of plastic oddments called "Toys-'Я'-Us."

There is no way I can describe the palpable despair emanating from all the adult earthlings in that place. Although they did appear to go there voluntarily, they clearly felt trapped. There was a grim look of resignation and mortification on all of their faces as they made their apparently painful selections from the hideously bountiful shelves and mumbled to themselves, "I can't believe I'm buying this."

And yet as they'd collide with other carts crammed with "Michael Jackson" dolls and assorted "GI Joe," "Care Bear," and "Cabbage Patch" paraphernalia, a real sense of camaraderie seemed to flourish among them. Bound together by some inexplicable mandate to pander to the demands of little earthlings, two mothers actually embraced with great compassion as they each reached for a talking "Knight Rider" car in a box that read "El Carro Habla Español." More to follow.

Day 3: The tension mounts. Yesterday I wandered the halls of an impressive edifice called Institute for Psychoanalysis. There were many small rooms there. And all the rooms were filled with couches. And all the couches were filled with people lying down and talking to a seemingly mute second person. And all the people were saying the same thing. "It happens every year. She always comes to visit at Christmas. I just don't think I can handle mother's visit again this year, Doc." It was very strange, Leader. All the Docs said the same thing, too—"Uh huhhh . . ."

Day 4: The more I'm here, the less clear things become. The earthlings seem to have coalesced into two distinct camps. One camp is made up of earthlings who can only operate in an ambience of full-throttle panic. They are called the "I haven't even started" camp. The other camp is made up of earthlings who are inordinately relieved. Not peaceful, but relieved. They are called the "I'm finally done" camp. But as I said, whatever it is that they are done with still hasn't brought them much peace. Both camps walk around saying the same thing, though. They say, "Merry Christmas." I'm not really sure what it means.

But I'm not sure if they know, either.

New Year's Nonobservance

Someone told me that tonight is New Year's Eve.

I smiled nonchalantly when I heard that. Because, you see, I've taken New Year's Eve off the list of Holidays to Be Observed. And once you take it off, it is no longer a problem.

I know there are supposedly people out there who put on long black gowns and have men in tuxedos pick them up and whisk them away to champagne-y places and they all have a divine time. But I have never been able to confirm this.

Especially the divine time part.

What I want to know is who invented New Year's Eve? I mean I know Pope Gregory XIII invented our current calendar. And I know that after December 31 it is obvious that we have to start with January all over again. But who is responsible for the creation of New Year's Eve?

More specifically, who invented the Frolic Imperative of New Year's Eve? Who came up with the concept that anything less than gala, anything less than wondrous, anything less than festive simply would not do for the evening of December 31?

Over the years New Year's Eve has become like fifty-two Saturday nights rolled into one. And it has imposed a ton of pressure on us to a) have plans, b) have plans with someone terrific, and c) have a terrific time executing these plans with this terrific person. Now most of us can usually manage to pull of a). But b) and c) have historically been the real killers. (Of course b) and c) are the real killers even when it's not New Year's Eve.)

But on New Year's Eve, you would always feel even crummier than usual about it. For instance, think of the ten most rotten fix-ups you've had in your life. Surely at least half of them have taken place on New Year's Eve. That's because New Year's Eve has been the one night you felt so leperlike for sitting home that you'd actually accept a date with someone who was clearly substandard.

And the worst part is, even if you've got a perfectly acceptable date (such as your boyfriend, girlfriend, or spouse), the pressure isn't off for New Year's Eve. You are still stuck with the mandate to Have an Extraordinarily Wonderful Time. Therefore if the two of us aren't invited to a couple of parties, you begin to panic and wind up doing something incredibly creepy. And you find yourself in the dining room of some hotel out by the airport where for $65 dollars a person you can eat a well-done filet mignon, dance to the lilting tunes of some suburban Laurence Welk, and sing "Should Old Acquaintance Be Forgot" with a room full of strangers at midnight. This is no way to launch your next 365 days.

But once you realize that the only really perfect New Year's Eve was the first one—when your parents finally let you stay up until midnight and watch Times Square on the tube—then you can do what I did. Just put New Year's Eve right up there on your list of unobserved holidays. Before you know it, it will just be another Flag Day.

NO, THERE AIN'T NO CURE FOR THE SUMMERTIME BLUES

The Family That Walkmans Together

'Tis the end of yet another fabulous family vacation on wheels. You pull into the garage, survey your crumpled family members (none of whom are speaking to each other by now), scrutinize the mounds of refuse that fill the interior of your vehicle, and swear to yourself—as you do every year—that you will never set foot in *this* car with *these* people for *that* many miles EVER AGAIN! Car trips do not do beneficial things for family dynamics.

No matter how large the car, no matter how swell the family, no matter how thrilling the destination, put any four people in a four-wheeled vehicle for more than four hours and you know the true meaning of torture. There are no exceptions. And yet we still have this mythical ho-ho-ho, over-the-river-and-through-the-woods expectation when we all clamor into our trusty automobile on the morning of summer vacation takeoff. We have this vision of immense Norman Rockwell coziness mushrooming between little Bobby and little Mindy Sue and ever-genial Mom and Dad as we tra-la-la our way through the countryside doing all sorts of festive things like counting license plates and singing "I've Been Working on the Railroad" in three-part harmony.

Harmony, however, is not in long supply on car trips. Discord is. It's there from the moment you creep out of your driveway at 4 A.M. on the morning of departure, the car crammed with more paraphernalia than a tribe of Bedouins have when they break camp; a minimum of one child on antibiotics who should be home in bed;

one other child who simultaneously fastens his seat belt and inquires, "When are we going to get there?"; one very irate husband, who is crabbing because "someone" forgot to cancel the newspaper for the next two weeks; and the little woman, who because she's going on "holiday" has no responsibilities besides packing for most of the ride-ees, serving snackettes to most of the ride-ees, and being chief referee for the regulation ride-ee bickering.

And ride-ee bickering is real plentiful. Because car trips breed tedium. And tedium does not breed tranquility. Regardless of the ingenious efforts you've made to activity-up the little ones, by the time you have reached the distant environs of, say, your local schoolyard, they have tried everything once, pronounced it crashingly boring, want to know if it's their turn with the pillow yet, and can they have a Twinkie and a root beer even though it's only five in the morning. With 683 miles to go, it's no fun to start discussing the merits of Twinkie-rationing with small people and to realize that the $23 you spent on books, crayons, and hand-held video games was basically for naught and that you are in for approximately ten hours of dissension.

The theory behind the car trip myth is that it's possible to keep children and adults of various ages interested in and amused by the same activities while traveling in a containerized environment. This of course is a fairly futile endeavor when you consider that outside the automotive cocoon the family members share a minimum of common interests. If they did, there would be no warfare over which station would be emanating from the radio instead of the eternal battle between all-news, all-love ditties, all-rock, and all-sports. If they did, it might be possible to play an occasional game of Twenty Questions—except most 1980s grown-ups have never heard of Prince and most 1980s kids have never heard of Clark Gable.

Which is why there is only one solution to car travel *en famille*. It is the *Chacun-à-Son*-Walkman School of Automotive Travel. And if you look around at the folks on the highways this summer, it is clearly quite the rage. Five people in a squalor-strewn car, each sporting earphones, each plugged in to the world of their choice, and each oblivious to the other four.

Hardly the Rockwellian definition of the family vacation. But after years of falsely hearty choruses of "They Built the Ship *Titanic*," at least now the family that drives their trip together has a chance to survive their trip together. If they don't run low on batteries.

The Price Is Never Right

This is a public service announcement. It is being issued in the hopes that we will not make the same mistake this summer that we make every summer when we plan our vacations. This summer let's try and really consider the high cost of trying to save money on vacation. I'm talking about the should-you-stay-at-the-Holiday-Inn or should-you-stay-with-Mary-and-Sam decision.

You inevitably choose the latter. It seems so economically wise. But it never really works out that way. Because you always pay. Sometimes out of your pocket, and even more often out of your psyche. But you always pay.

For starters, should you decide to go the Mary-and-Sam route, there's the proverbial we're-so-grateful-in-advance-for-your-hospitality house gift. This tends to be excruciatingly painful to select because you have never seen, or can never remember, Mary's basic household colors and motif. If it is delft blue and traditional, you inevitably have brought them something chrome and high tech. If it is Italian Modern and monochrome, you inevitably have brought them something rustic and red. And the something you bring always fits right into their lifestyle—like a great-looking set of steak knives which Mary and Sam would be very wild about if they didn't happen to be vegetarians. These gifts are always a big success. Just like the obligatory ones for the kids of Mary and Sam. There is no shopping task more odious (except buying a present for your mother-in-law) than figuring out what someone else's three-year-old boy and seven-year-old girl would consider to be amusing play-things. Thus, before you have even crossed the threshold chez Mary and Sam, you have spent major dollars for a plethora of presents that will probably be objets de trash in only a matter of weeks.

Secondly comes the food situation. They don't want to impose their vegetarian standards on you (which is helpful since you've never quite figured out what to do with an inert piece of tofu), so Mary has thoughtfully prepared some carnivore cuisine—boiled chicken. Three nights in a row of boiled chicken. You suggest on night three that you would like to take everybody out to a restaurant, but they absolutely will not hear of it—you are their *guests* . . . So you lie awake at night trapped in your host's hospitality and tormented by lurid dreams of pastrami on rye. It is not wise to remind yourself at this point that this is not exactly the way you planned to spend your vacation.

Not only are you starving, but you're sweltering. When Mary and Sam offered you bed and board, they neglected to mention that they live in the only house in Phoenix that doesn't have air-conditioning. It's bad for the cat. And when you accepted their offer of bed and board, you neglected to mention that you are allergic to cats. So you are starving, sweltering . . . and sneezing. Also, you are real embarrassed. The Q-tip you tossed down their idiosyncratic commode has caused it to clog up so you get to avail yourself of the pleasant task of using another family's plunger and, when that doesn't work, paying for the plumber. This is another point where it is unwise to remind yourself that this is not exactly the way you had planned to spend your vacation.

Listen, vacations are for lolling about, for indulgence, and for breaking out of the household routine. How can you break out of the household routine if you get locked into somebody else's? Who wants to go on vacation and feel obliged to wipe up the sink? Who wants to go on vacation and listen to someone else's version of great music or have to be kind to someone else's version of great kids?

In the end, it's just too costly to try and save money by not staying in a hotel. And anyway, when else but on a vacation are you ever going to have the pleasure of two towels a day?

Blessed Be the
Window Units

In the summer, the world divvies up into two fundamental types. Reasonable people. And the people who HATE air-conditioning. Or . . . shall we say, people who SAY they hate air-conditioning. It is my personal belief that it is impossible to have the minimum amount of functioning brain cells and actually really HATE air-conditioning.

Anybody with even a modicum of intelligence knows that air-conditioning was given to us as God's little testament that he still hasn't retired from the miracle biz. For several millennia, all God's children (with the exception of those banished to the tundra) were obliged to sweat on a serious basis at least several nights a year.

Heat waves are fundamentally vile little events that do nothing to enhance either your physical or emotional outlook. Your hair glomps into soggy, matted ringlets, your clothes acquire a socially unacceptable fragrance, and your normally benign personality takes a fast downward veer toward homicidal maniac.

Now humans have handled heat waves during some periods of history with more grace than during others. For instance, you can just imagine how ornery a heat wave must have made everyone, say, in the Middle Ages before they even had lemonade and tuna fish salad. And folks were sitting there just rusting out the inside of their armor.

God could have given us the air conditioner right then and there, but he decided to wait until we would really appreciate it. So he gave us a few more truly rotten centuries, with all kinds of revolutions every other week. And if it wasn't a plague, it was people getting drowned trying to discover Atlantic City and the rest of America. And then there was that nasty business of the Civil War, followed only a few decades later by World War I and the stock market crash. By then it was definitely time for a little divine intervention to perk up morale.

So by the mid-1930s we got the air conditioner. Granted, on a scale of miracles, it's no parting of the Red Sea, but it's not exactly chopped liver, either. I mean here we are with this major piece of technological wonderment that makes it possible on a sweltering ninety-degree day for a person to actually perform minor tasks like breathing.

And yet we are confronted with this astounding aberration— These perverse people who insist that they prefer to gasp and choke and sweat and faint and piously announce, "If there's one thing I can't stand it's fake air."

Oh please. I mean Daylight Savings Time is fake time, isn't it? Most of us have fake fibers on our backs, fake flavors in our food, fake flowers in our powder rooms . . . Fake air is just God's little way of offering us a bit a respite from some genuinely disgusting torpor.

So if you're one of those people out there sanctimoniously sweating your way through summer, I've got a little piece of advice for you . . . don't look a gift horse in the BTUs.

Dear Little Camper

For months now, you've been telling the kid that he is gonna have A GREAT TIME. That's what summer camp is for. And you would wax rhapsodic about campfires reeking of good fellowship, baseball games with no pressure from all us neurotic Little League parents, good ole-fashioned swimming in the secluded northern lake, and building wonderful memories with boys from all over America. Look at it this way, kid, you told him, it's a month-long birthday party up in the Michigan woods.

And for the most part, the kid actually buys your program. However, there are certain arenas of understandable hesitation. This is a child who has never been away from home without you for more than a grand total of four entire nights—and that was only when he was away visiting his grandmother. Thus, he is a trifle uneasy about twenty-eight consecutive days in the company of no one who shares his last name. But you manage to convince him that time flies when you're having fun.

He is also a bit distressed to hear that no phone calls are allowed unless it is a dire emergency. You smile buoyantly and promise him that the U.S. mails are perfectly adequate means of maintaining contact.

The kid is also concerned that he may get homesick. But again, with the serenity of a Mr. Rogers and the authority of Dr. Joyce Brothers you reassure him that this is but a momentary possibility, and that he will spend the rest of his time absolutely jubilant about this first overnight camp experience. By the time you get done pitching him, he's so fired up, he even sews on most of his own name tags.

You can barely believe your good fortune as you drive north Sunday morning to deliver him to camp. You've done such a good job that the kid is actually talking about staying an extra four weeks. A working mother's fantasy.

You pull into the campgrounds and are surrounded by a gaggle of hearty-counselor types. These are the responsible, well-balanced youths who will hold your kid's life in their hands for the next four weeks. You feel just fine about all of them. Except the one sleeping in the bed next to your kid, who runs into the cabin every now and then to put some Jergens Lotion on, so his hands don't get chapped. The bed next to your kid?

You unpack the kid's duffel while he heads off to take his swimming test. Except it gets rained out. A huge, dark, ominous thunderstorm has come up, so there's nothing to do but wait until lunch. Some of his bunkmates who knew each other from last year have reunioned-up and headed for the mess hall.

It's time for you to leave. The last you saw of him, he was sitting alone on his damp, unmade bed, a ten-watt bulb throwing a glimmer of light in the storm-darkened cabin, waiting for someone to say to him, "Let's go to lunch."

The next morning the lady behind the counter says to you, "Your son go to camp this weekend?" How did she guess? "Oh that's no guess," she tells you. "I've been working at the post office twenty years. It's 9:05 on the third Monday in June, you're mailing two letters, and, honey, you just got the look."

Sometimes you wonder: How do kids do it? How do they manage to make you thoroughly miserable when they're with you and thoroughly miserable when they're not?

Vacation by Lottery

On the list of fundamentally doomed endeavors, The Family Vacation has to rank right up there. That is because the successful family vacation is based on what they call *compromise*.

Compromise is something people write about. It does not work well in real life. It is a concept. A nice concept—sort of like the tooth fairy or world peace or taut thighs. But throw four people and one map inside a moving vehicle, and there is no way on God's green earth that they are going to want to head for the same destination.

Therefore, in order to compromise you pick a fifth destination, one that nobody really wants to go to, but it at least has the advantage of not being the first choice of any of the four passengers. That is how you landed up in Toad Suck, Arkansas, last summer.

This year, in an effort to avert the annual abortive attempt to be fair to everybody by pleasing nobody, a family lottery will be held. Each person has been asked to submit his ideal holiday. Thus, instead of trying to compromise, and coming up with a vacation plan that is basically unsatisfactory to four people, a winner will be picked. This way instead of everyone feeling cheated, only three people will feel cheated and one person might actually have a good time. A revolutionary concept to say the least.

Submission #1. The Husband. He has never quite understood why anyone would want to go anywhere but fishing. To be married to a person whose fundamental idea of paradise is getting up in the middle of the night to dig worms, stand knee-deep in subarctic water, and eviscerate slippery, smelly silver things is not a particularly encouraging thing. After all, you picked this person out from all the rest.

Submission #2. The Pom-Pon Girl. She wants to drive up the East Coast from Washington to Boston. You are dazzled. The child has finally acquired an appreciation for history. You can see it now —the Lincoln Memorial, the Liberty Bell, the Boston Harbor . . . Wrong. That's not exactly what she had in mind. She wants to go to D.C. to see the first night of the Springsteen concert and then shoot up to Manhattan to go to Bloomies, watch a taping of Ole Dave Letterman, and then head north to Filene's original bastion in Boston for a final shopping orgy . . .

Submission #3. The Kid. He's into theme trips. So what he proposes is that you hit every major amusement park in a two-hundred-mile radius, and include sidetrips to culturally significant video arcades and waterslides.

Submission #4. The Mom. The Mom's ideal trip is real simple. Being a totally selfless person, like most moms, she wants nothing other than to please each of the other three. Therefore, her ideal vacation is to have the Dad, the Kid, and the Pom-Pon Girl all go do exactly what they want. She wouldn't mind. Honest. Just as long as she didn't have to go along.

She's just sure she could manage all alone in her own house with no rock and roll blasting, no laundry to do, no fights over the television, no cooking, no car pooling, and no marketing. She's just sure that she'd be just fine actually having her very own house all to herself. Because once everyone vacates, there isn't a mom in the world who wouldn't have the vacation of her life.

And she wouldn't even have to pack.

Welcome Home

There's a real defective aspect to vacations.

The defective aspect is that you have to come home. Actually, the defective aspect is not so much *that* you have to come home, the defective aspect is *what you have to come home to.*

Suppose you had been traveling for a mere twenty-six straight hours on your way back from a one-week vacation in the Far East? As I said, it was a vacation, so you left the kids at home with a sitter. And as I said, it was only one week, so what could go wrong? And as I said, it was a mere twenty-six hours of sardine-ified economy class air travel, so when you arrive at long last at your very own front door, you are not in the mood for anything that does not look like a pillow and your very own bed.

But hark! What should you spot all shiny and silver jauntily perched on the hedge? Is it a piece from the fender of your brand new don't-you-dare-drive-this-while-I'm-gone car? Yes, indeed, it is. A special welcome home from your very own teenager.

And a mere precursor of what is to come when you walk in the door.

The first thing you spot is that your husband's absolute favorite, extremely valuable, extremely fragile, antique oriental rug is missing. You inquire in a calm, extremely collected fashion as to its whereabouts—O MY GOD! WHERE IS DADDY'S RUG??? (Daddy has remained in the Far East which enables you to make this inquiry—rather than watch him murder whoever might be responsible for the rug's disappearance.) The response you get is chilling. It seems that the canine had what is referred to in polite circles as "an accident" on it, and so the sitter rushed this extremely valuable, extremely fragile, antique oriental over to Wash-O-Rama Industrial Strength Rug Cleaning Service ("We Bleach Those Stains/No Grit Remains"). It is possible no marriage remains, either, depending on the condition of your rug.

All this in addition to the usual welcome home adorabilities: unopened newspapers piled knee high on the dining room table; seventeen pounds of junk mail; bills from every utility and department store known to mankind; a notice that you missed your dental appointment and are being charged for it; and a kitchen barren of any comestibles except Doritos and Diet Pepsi.

There's more. There's the bill for the emergency service call from the garbage disposal man. It had something to do with a chicken bone, and an item believed to have formerly been a valued part of your grandma's sterling silverware. There was the wet luggage rotting in the garage. It seems no one noticed there was a leak from the upstairs bathroom until the stench of the soggy luggage in the closet below began to be too much. And last, but not least, there was the water heater. Which apparently died a nonviolent and noble death about two hours after your plane took off.

Perhaps next year you'll be smarter. Next year you'll just send the house on vacation. It'll be cheaper.

MIXING IT UP WITH THE SEE-LEBS

Déjà-McGuire

Tears of immense joy were drizzling down my cheeks. I could not believe what I was reading. The McGuire Sisters are coming back! The McGuire Sisters! The quintessential white bread darling girl singing trio of all time. Homespun, huggable, and hygienic beyond belief, those "gals" out-Doris Dayed Doris Day in Full Fifties Wholesomeness.

When I was ten years old, there was almost nothing better than being sick on a school day and getting to curl up in bed listening to Arthur Godfrey yosh around between Lipton Tea commercials, with Julius La Rosa and the McGuire Sisters. One hour with squeaky clean Dorothy, Phyllis, and Christine and I felt I'd just witnessed the most glamorous, sophisticated of grown-up worlds. Morning radio seemed very racy.

What I didn't know from racy. Ask any ten-year-old kid who's home sick in bed today and trying to catch an hour of morning TV. He's got a choice between sitcom reruns, a full frontal view of penile implant surgery being featured on a show about impotence, a "noted sex authority" explaining with great aplomb that "size doesn't count," or the confessions of several housewives enthusiastically explaining their surefire methods of turning on their husbands. (We're not talking wearing a pretty dress and cooking his favorite meal methods; we're talking technique, positions, apparatus, and all the things Mama taught you never to talk about.)

I think we have OD'd on candor. The line that once existed

between what you talk about in a public forum and what you don't talk about has been demolished. It is very bizarre to watch total strangers stand up and tell a TV camera things that are almost too personal to hear from your best friend. What prompts a person to tell the world at large that her first husband was "too small" and her current husband is "too big." This is embarrassing to hear.

Have we become embarrassed about feeling embarrassed? I'm tired of trying to act unruffled when what I really want to do is throw my hands over my ears, gasp with unabashed horror, and say, "Please, please, no more." Of course we can always turn it off, or switch channels, but the barrage of free-floating frankness is relentless. And it makes me wish it was a bit more fashionable to be a little more private about our privates.

Maybe mine is just the despair of one lone regressive, sexually repressed woman. But I doubt it. Imagine sending off for tickets to one of these talk shows, waiting all these months for the big day, hoping against hope for Tom Selleck or Liz, and then getting the gamey confessions of the lady in the row in front of you. Wouldn't life be a bit lovelier if there were a few delicate topics left? But delicate has gone a bit by the boards given our contemporary mind-set of candor for candor's sake. In our ever-vigilant pursuit of the unminced word, a lot of us have forgotten how to blush.

There is nothing wrong with the anatomical words for our you-know-whats. But even for the sophisticates among us, to hear Those Words every third sentence over the airwaves has to be a somewhat jarring way to start off our day. Which is why I'm so excited about the McGuire Sisters. Those girls know how to keep a morning conversation nice and benign.

Do me a favor. Don't bother calling me the morning they're on discussing how they lost their virginity. I'll be out slitting my wrists.

Picnic with Porn Queen

Today we answer a pressing question . . . can an actual porno queen and an actual suburban wife find a common meeting ground?

Seka, the "platinum princess of porn," has invited me to lunch. As porn queens go, the woman is unique. At least from the neck up. She's very bright and very beautiful. We are talking seriously terrific, good-enough-for-*Vogue* bones. Only for the past thirteen years it hasn't been her bones that the thirty-five-year-old has let the camera focus on. But I digress . . . We're going on a picnic. "Bring your bathing suit," says my hostess. "We'll go up on the roof."

Do you know the kind of nerve it would take to appear next to Seka in a bathing suit? We are rained out. I always knew there was a God.

So we picnic in her gray and mauve dining room hung with four Erté etchings. The apartment is very tasteful. Her pink silk and linen suit is very tasteful. The pâté and prosciutto lunch is very tasteful. Not only is everything tasteful. It's normal. Heartbreakingly normal. The TV is humming with "All My Children," there are no mirrors on the bedroom ceiling (eat your hearts out, guys), no manacles on the headboard, and the book resting next to the phone is not the *Kama Sutra*, it's Leo Rosten's *The Joys of Yiddish*.

This strikes me, a woman whose ethnic roots are mired in gefilte fish and matzo balls, as surprising. So I ask this former churchgoing Presbyterian why she likes Yiddish. "Because it's incredibly expressive." So what is her favorite expression? *"Rachmones."* This is not a word I know. "It means compassion," she explains patiently.

I figured I'd learn a thing or two from Seka; I just didn't think it would be Yiddish.

I learned we have a lot in common: 1) We both hate doing laundry. Seka, however, has managed to turn this into a profitable enterprise by doing a healthy mail-order business selling her used unmentionables. 2) We both used to be fat in high school. The now 118-pound Seka weighed in at 160 junior year. Which still didn't prevent her from being elected Miss Hopewell High, back home when she was just plain Dottie in Hopewell, Virginia. 3) We both have Certain Rules. For instance Seka states emphatically that she wouldn't sleep with two men in the same day. Like most suburban wives, I, too, have always felt this to be prudent.

I also learned there was a lot she didn't have in common with the average suburban wife: 1) Seka was a virgin when she got married. "I was only eighteen, and had been an athlete, not a cheerleader in high school. I didn't date a lot. I went from being a jock to being married. The first night I locked myself in the bathroom I was so terrified." The marriage only lasted a year and a half. (The terror, as anyone knows who has seen her films, couldn't have lasted long at all. 2) The longest she has ever gone without sex was for six months—three years ago. Now it gets bad in suburbia, but not that bad. 3) She calls her mom four or five times a week. Now how many of us suburban wives can claim to be as attentive?

We talked clothes (she adores Chanel suits and Maud Frizon shoes); pets (she has Yvonne the poodle and Mike the cockatoo); books (she's dyslexic, so it's slow going); and solitude. That night, for instance, the porn queen was staying home alone to watch TV.

The afternoon flew. And when we said good-bye, we kiss-kissed the air to the side of each other's face. Just like ladies leaving a bridge party. Very tentatively she said to me, "It would be nice to go out to dinner sometime." I said that would be great. And realizing there's not such a chasm after all between an X-rated woman and a woman who takes her car pool responsibilities seriously, I asked if she might like to come home one night with me out to the suburbs.

"Sure." And then she adds, with a major wink, "I give great grill."

Paul Newman: When Blue Eyes Meet Four Eyes

This is a two-part column. Part one deals with reality, and part two deals with fantasy. Since I am one of those people who likes to eat dessert first, let's start out with the fantasy part.

I expect if you asked a random sampling of women what male movie star they'd most like to meet, and I'm talking WOMEN here, not sweet young things who think Matt Dillon counts, you'd probably get a two-way split between Mr. Robert Redford and Mr. Paul Newman. I personally would cast my vote for Paul Newman. Because I've always felt Paul Newman and I have a lot in common. We both take our spaghetti sauce seriously and we both were born in Cleveland.

In fact Paul Newman used to hang out at my father's store. This, of course, was before he became PAUL NEWMAN, but was just a kid. I only know this story because once (after he became PAUL NEWMAN and my family had moved out to Los Angeles) he ran into my dad and mom at the airport. And, as family lore has it, he smiled at my dad and said, "Aren't you Mr. Wade?" And my old man, impervious to the fact that my mother was hyperventilating because PAUL NEWMAN had come over, said simply, "Yeah. I remember you. Aren't you the kid I used to toss out of my record store?" I've always felt this anecdote would be a great little conversation opener if I ever got shipwrecked on an island with Paul Newman. Now, moving right along to reality . . .

There are in the twentieth century marketplace a few wondrous inventions that have radically enhanced the appearance of women who might otherwise be considered less than smashing. For some, padded bras made all the difference in the world. For others it was braces or perhaps just the right shade of Miss Clairol. These seemingly insignificant bits of technological wonderment have worked miracles for the individual self-esteem of millions.

In my particular case, it was the invention of contact lenses that has made me unafraid to show my face in public. I know there are people who claim a woman can look great in glasses, but most of those people are probably related to opticians. Or to Sophia Loren. For a person as myopic as myself, the minimum thickness of a pair of specs is about one-quarter inch. On a scale of clarity, one-quarter-inch-thick glasses make Coke bottle bottoms look like Baccarat crystal.

It's not easy to admit one's entire personal identity is tied up in a pair of tiny, tinted plastic lenses, but I am convinced that if contacts hadn't been invented I'd have wound up doing something serious and sensible instead of having all this fun as a journalist.

And journalism is the reason that fantasy and reality have finally collided. It seems that I have recently been given the magazine assignment of my dreams—a profile on Paul Newman. Of course he hasn't agreed to it yet. But the salient issue is that exactly forty-eight hours after getting this assignment, my opthamologist told me that I might have to give up contact lenses for the next few months. Thus the one time in my entire life I may actually get to meet Paul Newman, I will be trapped behind the thickest, most impenetrable, most geeky pair of glasses in the world.

I thought you might want that one for your The Lord Giveth and The Lord Taketh Away file . . .

Ricky

This is not a column I ever intended to write.

Because I never intended to be sitting here, a full-fledged adult, grieving, actually grieving over Ricky Nelson.

But here I am—stunned, saddened, and surprised that I'm feeling so heartsick.

After all, I'm a forty-two-year-old woman. Fully aware that in the annals of Twentieth Century Talent, Ricky Nelson would probably not make anybody's list in the top two hundred. But so what.

He was Ricky Nelson.

There was a time in my life when Ricky Nelson was everything to me. Everything. He was the only obsession I've ever had. No one before or since has ever touched me in the same way. When Elvis died I felt sad. When John Lennon was murdered I felt sad. But not like this.

Ricky Nelson was my youth. He was elaborate fantasies woven and rewoven every night before I fell asleep. He was the walls of my bedroom, the main topic of my conversation, the recipient of weekly letters, the excuse I had for not being nice to the pimply boys in seventh grade. He was the intensity, the passion, the adoration that you can only feel when you are thirteen and will never get any closer to the object of your affections than the pages of *Photoplay*. He was the only man in my life who never had any flaws. We never even had our first fight.

Actually my first fight was with his father. I was sixteen years old and living in Los Angeles, and by then the thirteen-year-old's obsession had faded to mere infatuation. So I used to drive over and stake out the Nelson house in hopes of seeing my guy. No such luck. But after three or four weeks of this, Ricky's father grew a bit testy. I have the unique distinction of actually inciting the benign Mr. Ozzie Nelson to profanity. I got Ozzie Nelson to use the s-word.

It wasn't until ten years later that I actually met Ricky. By then he was Rick and I was a married woman working in Washington, D.C. He was playing at The Cellar Door and I couldn't get a soul to come along with me to see him. So I went alone. The cabaret was only about half full so it wasn't too hard to wangle an invite backstage between sets. He was wonderful. Snappy conversation was never his long suit, but he was sweet, and soft, and even laughed when I told him the story about Ozzie. I knew he'd dealt with a trillion of me, but for me that night was definitely a Major Moment.

I met him again three years ago. He was playing the O'Hare Regency and I was free-lancing for *Cosmopolitan*. I wanted to do a piece on meeting your idol twenty-five years later. I thought it would make a great story. *Cosmo* didn't.

The problem was Ricky Nelson spent most of his life being sort of a joke. Once the fifties were over and the music got more complex, Ricky Nelson was relegated by some to smirk status. And everyone kept stashing him in the past. This man spent the whole second half of his life trying to break through a lot of people's insistence that he was only a musical artifact. *Cosmo* told me not to bother to write up the interview.

But I think they were wrong. Because for millions of us premenopausal women, he will always own a sliver of our hearts. We can't explain why. It wasn't just that he was criminally good-looking. Or appealingly aw-shucks shy. Or that he had the best lip curl in the world. Listen, his music was good. Not extraordinary, but good. Even so, we've always been made to feel a bit goofy for having adored him.

Only no more. I refuse to feel goofy for grieving. Now Ricky Nelson is gone.

And dammit, that hurts.

On Being Mistaken
for Catherine
Deneuve

One of the things you learn to accept in life is that you probably are not going to be stopped on the street because someone has mistaken you for Catherine Deneuve. Not even on one of your good days.

This is something that over the years you manage to live with.

And then one day that all starts to change. Well, perhaps it doesn't actually change, but you become aware that it could change at any minute. Because you have just seen a news photo of Catherine Deneuve that stops you dead in your tracks. You blink, you look again, but the camera does NOT lie . . . there they ARE! Catherine Deneuve has wrinkles! You can hardly believe it. But right there, three inches above her ethereal, serene, incredibly Deneuvian smile are bunches and crunches of unretouched eye wrinkles!

Your heart swells. Not with malice. You certainly don't wish this forty-four-year-old woman ill. You have no hard feelings toward this person, in spite of the fact that for two decades her personal face has managed to make your personal face look like chopped liver. No, you're just not the kind of girl who would carry a grudge against a woman who has pretty much set the curve on divine. No, your heart swells for another reason.

You suddenly love this woman. Catherine Deneuve doesn't even go out in the sun. But she has wrinkles. Catherine Deneuve has spent years advertising lotions and potions. But she has wrinkles. Catherine Deneuve can afford a lifetime supply of Retin-A and the best plastic surgeons in the world. But she has wrinkles. How can you not love her?

I mean it was one thing to gaze upon the cragged face of Lillian Hellman. Lillian was a playwright, she wasn't famous for her beauty. In fact cragging up gave her more credibility. Same with Georgia O'Keefe or with Martha Graham. They were famous for their art, not for their faces. So they could let their faces crag up and it was definitely the right look for them. It's different for Catherine Deneuve. Because although she does act, Catherine Deneuve is basically famous for her beauty. So the concept of Catherine and the concept of crags have always seemed mutually exclusive.

But there they are, merged, in this news photo. A photo I personally feel should be taped to the mirror of every post-forty-year-old girl who invests large sums in potions and lotions. Because this is the ultimate good news photo. Because crow's-feet for crow's feet, puff for puff, splotch for splotch, you are at long last beginning to look more and more like Catherine Deneuve.

I mean it really does give a girl pause. It really does force a girl who has been considering a tad of plastic surgery to ask the pivotal question: Who do you really want to look like—a twenty-three-year-old version of you, or a forty-four-year-old version of Catherine Deneuve?

And you cancel your appointment.

Grandpa Ringo

Ringo Starr is a grandfather. I'd say as far as stop-you-dead-in-your-track news tidbits go, that one pretty much sets the curve. I suppose it depends what decade of your life you are in, but if, in fact, you are somewhere in the mid-three-o to mid-four-o zone, this is indeed a killer statistic.

None of us expected Ringo to stay young forever. God knows we haven't managed to do it. And in fact, there's been a certain pleasure, even comfort, in watching all the strident, adamant, irrepressible sixties folk mature and mellow into mid-life. Jerry Rubin, Jane Fonda, even the perennially pixie Paul, that quintessential Beatle boychick, have all seasoned and softened into very reasonable adults. But Ringo is the first one of us who's had the audacity to go ahead and become a *grandfather*.

One can take some solace in pointing out that this doesn't necessarily mean Ringo is *old*. It simply means that he started making babies about one second after he was biologically able to and apparently so did his progeny. Ringo's son, Zak Starkey, the culprit who is causing this entire identity crisis, is all of nineteen years old. Had this kid kept a better handle on his hormones, this entire issue could have been postponed for at least a few years—when we no doubt would have accepted the concept of Grandpappy Ringo more gracefully.

Yeah, sure. We never would have accepted it gracefully. That's because while most of us have accepted that we're no longer young, we have not accepted that we're actually getting old. For instance, most adults do not get all depressed and crazy just because they require the assistance of a teenage person to name and identify everyone but Harry Belafonte and Ray Charles in the *We Are the World* video. We accept that musical tastes and stars are made by the young and that that is no longer the category for which we qualify.

But that hardly means we are ready to leap wholeheartedly into grandparent-dom. Just because we're no longer in the vanguard of rock, does that mean we are ready to crawl into our rockers?

When Paul Newman turned sixty, it was tough to believe. But then Paul Newman has always been older, so there was a sense of reasonability about it. It didn't boggle the mind like this. But Ringo is only forty-four at this writing, he's OUR age. And even more importantly, the concept of Ringo, the core of Ringo, his essential Ringo-ness is all hooked into not just youth, but brash, irreverent, flagrant youth. Our youth. And now he's a gramps.

My children do not understand why this news is making me crazy. Why should they understand? Ringo Starr has always been old to them. I have always been old to them. And, of course, they have always been young. Smugly, securely, invincibly young.

So I tried to put it in context. "Let me put it this way," I said. "How would you feel if it was 2005 and you were at a restaurant and you saw Madonna?"

"Great," they said.

"And she had liver spots all over her hands???"

One brought me flowers and the other brought me tea and toast.

Bill Veeck: Beyond Baseball

Let 'em all talk about Bill Veeck and baseball. Bill Veeck wasn't baseball to me.

Let 'em talk about Bill Veeck and legend. Bill Veeck wasn't legend to me. He was an ever-since-I-can-remember-close-as-family part of my life.

He first captured my heart in 1948. I guess it was the same 1948 that the Cleveland Indians won the World Series. What did I know. I was four years old. And Bill Veeck happened to be my parents' best friend. He was the muse and the center of "The Jolly Set," a cyclone of grown-ups who leeched more fun out of every twenty-four-hour day than Cleveland had ever seen. Or has ever seen since.

My mom and dad adored Bill, and he adored them back. And one day (or night, it was probably night)—he presented me with the hugest, huggiest, most pinkly elaborate baby doll ever. And I didn't even like dolls. In fact I resolutely resisted dolls. But this one? Who could resist a doll picked out by Bill Veeck? The guy who was great at picking ball players was a great doll picker, too. So first of all, Bill Veeck is frilly pink dolls to me.

Second of all, he is a bit of childhood loneliness. He was the reason my parents always took long trips away. Because once he left Cleveland and began messing up our address book with different numbers in Tucson and New Mexico and Chicago and Easton, my parents always took off. Who could resist an invitation from Bill

Veeck? There was too much craziness to be had, insights to be gained, warmth to bask in, and magic to rub up against.

Like the time Bill Veeck turned my old man into a cowboy. My dad, who was a textile salesman in real life, had always wanted to be . . . I don't know. Anything but a textile salesman. He wanted to be Charles Lindbergh, or Ernest Hemingway, or something a little more outrageous than Willy Loman. So he took a month off between engagements in the garment industry, went out to Bill's New Mexico ranch, and drove cattle for a month. Bill Veeck may have given the world its first American League black ball player and its first midget batter, but he also gave it its first Jewish cowboy from Cleveland.

Bill also gave me my daddy back. Sort of. When I lost my dad ten years ago and then moved to Chicago a few years later, he was the one who gave me the encouragement, and the chutzpah and a go-for-it speech when I decided in the middle of my life to actually become a writer. He was the one who called and said "great piece" on the occasional Sunday when my column was only just a little above average. And he was the one who made room in his heart, despite having nine of his own children, to be proud of one more.

The best thing that Bill Veeck gave me, though, was a glimpse into extraordinarily clean and unconfused loving. I have never seen a marriage like the one he and Mary Frances Veeck put together. I have never seen two people woven quite so tightly, so finely tuned, so visibly one, yet so private about some of their oneness. I have never seen that kind of mutual protection, mutual respect, that sense of actually *being* in concert with another person. I think Bill and Mary Frances Veeck did marriage and loving better than just about anyone I've ever known. Of course who could resist loving, and being loved, by Bill Veeck?

Four years ago when I turned forty, Bill made me a wonderful mobile and wrote me an even more wonderful letter. He did it on the computer, which was pretty newfangled for a hunt-and-peck type. In fact, while he wrote the text on the damn thing, he clearly wasn't ready to deal with its editing functions, so all the corrections are in green, felt-tip pen.

Here's what some of that letter said: "They're saying that now you've made it to forty, you're good for forty more. But they're dealing in years, not time, and years don't mean much. Years are finite. Time is infinite. It is time I am writing you about.

"By now you'll realize you never have enough of it to do all the things you want, can, and plan to do. So time, in the second half becomes more precious, more fleeting. I do not know why this should be so, but it is. Use it wisely. The time remaining. Use it with joy, with a sense of accomplishment, of fulfillment. But above all, use it. Don't let it use you or slip by unnoticed. There will always be too much undone, unlearned, unfinished, unsaid. So taste, savor, and enjoy every possible minute, every possible second."

I don't know anyone who wrung more living out of life than Bill Veeck. That is his legacy.

To say we'll miss him, doesn't begin to cover it.

The Rob Lowe-down

The mother of a teenage daughter exists for two reasons. To be ignored, and to be hated. Not really hated. Just hated enough to make the separating-out process a bit easier. The sort of God-my-mom-is-such-a-bitch sort of hate that along with rhinestone earrings and a pair of Guess? jeans are prerequisite equipment for the basic adolescent mode. This kind of hate is pretty much a pro-forma thing.

And at least 80 percent of the time you are rational enough not to take it personally.

However, there is that 20 percent of the time when you would give absolutely anything to score a couple of points with the kid. And one day, you find yourself in the position of being able to offer her nothing less than the moon. Rob Lowe is in town filming a movie and you are going to take her down to the set.

Rob Lowe, for those of you who have been in the gulag for the past few years, is what is known as major heartthob material. He is girl-beautiful, chronically elusive, and the mere mention of his name does weird things to the already raging hormonal levels of teenage girls.

Thus, you figure that transporting the teenager and her girl-friend downtown in rush-hour traffic, to stand on a movie set fifty feet from the illustrious Mr. Lowe, and possibly even get his auto-graph, will at least garner you a few days of civility from said teen-ager. Perhaps even warmth. Fool that you are.

Because what you realize when you are finally on the set, and the teen-squeals have been momentarily muffled, is that no teenage girl is going to really be content to simply *observe* the lovely Mr. Lowe. What each and every one is actually hoping for in her heart of buoyant hearts is that Rob Lowe will see her, be dumbstruck, stop whatever he is doing, saunter on over . . . and ask her to marry him. Or at least saunter on over and banter a bit. What is the point of seeing Rob Lowe without being able to return to school the next day and say "and then he said . . . and then I said . . ." It's a normal enough wish.

Only multiply it by hundreds. Hundreds of wishes, times hundreds of squealy girls, times hundreds of hormones and you get an idea of what Mr. Lowe is dealing with all day every day. Which is why it's not one bit surprising that when a couple of flitting, touching, giggling girlchicks follow Mr. Lowe off the set and into the coffee joint next door, he is something less than a Prince Charming toward them. He spent the preceding night having water dumped on his head until two or three in the morning, so he's got a rotten cold, and he just finished sloshing around in fake snow for another four or five hours, so "gracious" does not come easy for him at this moment.

Unfortunately, this is the only moment the teenchicks have with him. He doesn't insult them, but when the director comes in and says, "Hey, we can call the cops if these *brats* are bothering you," he just laughs. And starts to mock them. They are devastated.

Shatter. There goes the idol.

Shatter. There go their hearts.

And they rush outside to tell you What a Creep, What a Snot, What a Total Jerk, Rob Lowe Is in Real Life.

And you know deep in your heart they think It's All Your Fault.

ABOUT THE AUTHOR

Judy Markey was born in Cleveland, raised in Los Angeles, and now lives in a suburb of Chicago with one husband, two kids, two dogs, and two Volvos. In 1980, at the age of thirty-six, she began her writing career, and her work has since appeared in the *New York Times*, *Cosmopolitan*, *Woman's Day*, *New Woman*, and the *Chicago Sun-Times*. Her column is now syndicated by King Features.